pilgrimage

with the

Leprechauns

A True Story of a Mystical Tour of Ireland

Tanis Helliwell

Cover and all photographs by Tanis Helliwell

Library and Archives Canada Cataloguing in Publication
Helliwell, Tanis

Pilgrimage with the Leprechauns: A true story of a mystical tour of Ireland / by Tanis Helliwell.

ISBN 978-0-9809033-2-4

1. Leprechauns. 2. Spiritual life. 3. Helliwell, Tanis--Travel. 4. Ireland--Description and travel. I. Title.

GR549.H45 2010   398.21   C2010-900564-3

Published by Wayshower Enterprises

www.iitransform.com

Printed and bound in Canada

Dedication

This book is dedicated to all world servers who are working to heal the Earth and to bring love, peace, and wisdom to all.

Gudrun,

Blessings on Your path
& in your life

Tanis .

Acknowledgments

Although only my name appears as author, I wish to acknowledge my indebtedness to 'Lloyd' and others, who taught me about elementals. A special thank you to all members of the *Mystical Tour of Ireland* and my Irish friends whose identity I keep silent to ensure their privacy.

I thank all the people who read *Summer with the Leprechauns: A True Story* and who urged me to write another book with the leprechaun. It's been a long time coming, but here it is. Enjoy!

For their support and trust in me, my gratitude to the members of the International Institute for Transformation, who are committed to co-creating with elementals and humans to heal our Earth.

I owe especial thanks to Margaret, of Irish Adventure Tours (a pseudonym), who supported me both before and after the tour. I appreciated the editorial suggestions from Jenny Linley, Simon Goede, Ruth Dees, Janet Alred, Eva van Loon, Jennifer McBeath, Marielle Croft, Jill McBeath, Paul Horn, Ann Mortifee, and Monika Bernegg, my German translator. I'm also grateful for the patient encouragement and persistence of my agent and friend, Bob Silverstein, who insisted on many re-writes to find the balance between an amusing travel story and the lessons learned.

Lastly, I thank my mother, Margaret Helliwell, who gave me Irish blood and love of all things Irish. Blessings on your way.

Table of Contents

Whan that Aprille with his shoures soote

The droghte of March hath perced to the roote...

And small fowles maken melodye

That slepen al the nyght with open eye,

So priketh hem nature in hir corages.

Thanne longen folk to goon on pilgrimages.

Chaucer, *Canterbury Tales*, Prologue l. 1-9

pRefACe: A pIlGRIm's beARt

S ome years ago I lived in an old cottage in the village of Keel on the west coast of Ireland. I shared Crumpaun Cottage with a leprechaun and his family who had lived there for a very long time. The leprechaun befriended me and taught me about elementals, and especially about those, with whom he works, who are committed to co-create with like-minded humans in order to heal the Earth.

I was surprised at how deeply *Summer with the Leprechauns,* my book about that experience, touched the hearts of so many people who are interested in, and believe in nature spirits. Some have seen them, and many more have seen signs of them, or have felt them near. Thirty people from Europe and North America who believed in elementals, and wanted to experience them personally, registered for the *Mystical Tour of Ireland,* which I was leading. They and I both received an inner call to journey to Ireland and none of us realized, in our outer world, that we were committing to a deep inner pilgrimage. Quite the contrary. I have conducted three other mystical tours to Ireland, and had spent a year and a half organizing the tour, so I expected everything to run smoothly, almost like having a vacation.

Very little happened as I had planned, and by outer standards the *Mystical Tour of Ireland* was an unmitigated disaster. However, in terms of deep personal transformation, it was one of the most significant events of my life. Although each of us underwent a different inner journey, I can only relate my own personal experience, and some lessons I understand, only now, through writing this book.

I began, over twenty years ago, after living with the leprechaun family, to lead tours and pilgrimages taking people to sacred sites of the world to assist them with their transformation. These experiences remove us from the world of work, paying bills, and old ways of thinking. They even remove us from clutching to a past, or hoping for a future.

Pilgrimages are not meant to be easy for, if they were, no transformation would occur. The pilgrim is, in fact, often confronted by an ordeal, or a series of difficulties. Blisters on our feet, no food, or not seeing the sacred sites we yearn to visit are all outer ordeals. Just as important are the inner ordeals of frustration, anger, self-pity, and sadness that accompany our unravelling. In this way, we learn non-attachment to having things our way, as well as forgiveness, acceptance of what is, living in the present moment, and finding joy and peace in whatever happens.

Ultimately, the goal of pilgrimage is to arrive at our heart's centre. What do we find there and how do we interpret the answer? This answer may be profound, life changing, and so dramatic that we can no longer return to the life we led. The answer might as easily be a simple knowing that a mother's kiss, a sunset, a playful puppy is as important as a vision of Christ. Whatever the answer, we need to fully embrace and assimilate the inner and outer journey, while at the same time realizing that the pilgrimage never ends and that different lessons reveal themselves at different stages of our life.

It is not the destination so much as the focus of the journey that defines a pilgrim and, if you are travelling with a leprechaun and an assortment of other elementals, as we were doing, having a good sense of humour and a light heart is essential. The key to our pilgrimage in Ireland lies in understanding what the Irish call 'The Craic.' We journeyed through the Craic, and with the Craic, and we were having the Craic. Only the Irish can really understand the Craic, and I often think that they invented it. It is hard to give you a definition of the Craic, but a few words about it might point you in the right direction. The Craic sums up all life's experience—the good and the bad—that which can be understood and that which cannot.

The Craic cannot be pinned down and, when you try to do so, it joggles you out of your comfort zone and laughs at you. It is both the great cosmic joke and cosmic joker. The Craic is what lies between the 'this' and the 'that.' I often think of it as the crack—Craic—between the worlds, between the three-dimensional reality, in which humans spend their waking hours, and other dimensions. The Craic is magic. The Craic is unpredictable and certainly not dependable. It comes whenever it wants, and does whatever it can, to move us into deeper knowing and truth. The only approach a sane person can take towards the Craic is to surrender to it, as any resistance is futile.

The Craic is a mind-set that can be applied to almost any situation. I remember the occasion when my great-aunt Boots died after lying in a foetal position in bed for some months. My father, in a serious tone, was telling his brother Wilton the news when the Craic took over the conversation.

Asked by Wilton how Boots had died, my father replied, "Boots died of the crouch."

Hearing these words, my ninety-year-old Irish grandmother started cackling, which my Dad did not appreciate. Trying to recover his balance, he fell deeper into the Craic with his next words, "Boots will be married Monday."

It's very Irish to be able to laugh at death and my grandmother completely broke up at my father's last verbal error. This black humour is the Craic. If we love the Craic, we can find something amusing in uncomfortable, or even traumatic, events. When we flow with the *hungernot*

Craic, we are not victimized by a bad situation. The Irish have had plenty of bad situations throughout their history with famine, wars, and being regarded as lesser people by conquering races, so perhaps that is why they are able to laugh at the Craic.

Leprechauns, and elementals in general, excel at living and playing in the Craic and find joy and amusement there. Most humans, save the Irish, do not. The humans, who accompanied me on the *Mystical Ireland Tour,* received the experience of elementals that they had requested, but not always in a way that they, or I, could control. The leprechauns took us on a mighty journey with great Craic, and I, for one, will never be the same.

Ah, but perhaps I should back up and tell you a wee bit about leprechauns and elementals, the race to which leprechauns belong. Elementals, otherwise called nature spirits, the little people, and faeries, are real and every country has its stories and myths about them. For example, there are leprechauns in Ireland, trolls in Scandinavia, gnomes in Germany, *patuparehe* in New Zealand, *kappa* and *tengu* in Japan, and the *aluxuses* of the Mayan people of Central America. Mind you, elementals can travel around and even live outside their ancestral country, much as humans do, so you could see a troll in Canada and a gnome in New Zealand.

Sometimes, people see and hear elementals in the real world, and I receive countless letters and emails from countries around the world from individuals who have had these real-life encounters. However, because elementals, like angels and ghosts, are found in a lighter dimension than what most humans perceive, people more often see them with their psychic-sight.

I have been able to see beings in other dimensions since I was born. These include, but are not limited to, elementals, angels, and people who have died. In Ireland it's called having 'second sight' and this gift runs, by way of my mother, through the Irish side of my family. My family never spoke about our second sight and treated it matter-of-factly. It is a secret that we hid by calling it a 'good guess', or a 'hunch.'

I mention this 'second sight' now, as the story I am about to tell you will only make sense if you realize that I am conversing with a leprechaun that most people can neither see nor hear. The tour I'm describing in *Pilgrimage with the Leprechauns: A True Story of a Mystical Tour of Ireland* is one of great Craic, and can be enjoyed as an amusing Irish travel story, as a fount of information on nature beings, and as an inner journey of transformation.

To protect my fellow pilgrims and others, I have changed many of their names.

I hope you enjoy the pilgrimage and have good Craic!

Tanis Helliwell, St. Patrick's Day, March 2010

a joyful Craic

friendly Lucky

Clementals amusing in the Craic.

ᴛḃe Lepꞃecḣauɲ's Ϣessaᵹe

Whether you know it, or not, you have been called here: some by your ancestors whose blood flows in your veins, some to help elementals, some to heal our Earth, and some to be healed by her hands, heart, and voice, which we elementals hear.

We take you on a magical mystical tour full of fun, spontaneity in the moment, and openness to being your true selves. Yes, and even laughing at yourself, which we Irish call *'The Craic'*.

Surrender to the experience and you will find joy and be transformed.

Resist and make yourselves miserable. It is your choice. This is a healing journey!

Map of Mystical Tour of Ireland

Part I

Outer Pilgrimage by Bus

CHAPTER ONE

🍀

OFF TO A ROCKY START

I love Ireland: its green fields, rousing breeze and the feeling of magic and wonder that awaits you just below its surface. Although I've been there some thirteen times, I can never get enough and, like a child, I eagerly look forward to each new visit.

Then there's my leprechaun friend, who goes by the name of 'Lloyd' when dealing with curious humans. As the name 'Lloyd' in Welsh (a Gaelic language resembling Irish) means grey-haired, wise, sacred, and also connotes a restless energy, he chose a perfect name for himself to my way of thinking. During one of my earlier sojourns to the rugged west coast of Ireland, I lived with him and his family in a haunted cottage on Achill Island.

Lest you think that I'm loony-tunes, let me explain that it's well-known in Keel, the little village in which the leprechaun lives, that my cottage was haunted by the little people. The veil between this world and other dimensions is thin in the west of Ireland and more 'sightings' of the little people happen there than in other areas of Ireland.

Knowing my leprechaun friend and other nature beings is sometimes sheer bliss filled with magical adventures and other times, when I have expectations that are not met, it is sheer frustration. I am learning to flow in both states with equal ease and grace. At least, I

[handwritten margin notes: "Neben- bedeutung", "Aufent- halte"]

thought I was learning to do this until Lloyd took thirty leprechaun lovers and me on his topsy-turvy version of a tour to the sacred sites of Ireland.

In a carefree frame of mind I arrived in Dublin, checked into the hotel, and was greeted by a welcoming phone call by James, one of the owners of Gallows, the Irish tour company. I did not know at that time that Margaret, my tour contact in Canada, had a nickname for James that speaks volumes. It was 'The Lep', short for 'The Leprechaun', as James, both in his look and manner, reminded Margaret of an elemental. The fact that someone called 'The Lep' organized the tour might have alerted me that our tour would have some bends in the road. After all, we already had my leprechaun pal Lloyd coming with us, but with two leprechauns anything could happen.

The first morning dawned rainless, always a good sign in Ireland and, while checking out, I was warmly greeted by Helen and Molly, two women from 'across the water', as the Irish say of North Americans. Helen's a freckle-faced redhead with very much the Irish look about her. At the same time, she's a no-nonsense woman who works with the police back home, and has earned their respect through her clever mind and practical ideas. Molly's a wavy-haired brunette with almost black, all-seeing eyes. She's a happily married business consultant, with a couple of grown boys, who have just left the nest, giving her a chance to seek her dream of going to Ireland.

The three of us chatted together while awaiting our bus and, within a few minutes, a brand-spanking-new fifty-seater vehicle pulled up. The door opened and a friendly face peeked out.

"Hello, I'm Paddy O'Shea, yer driver," said a fortyish, average-built man with short-cropped hair and strong Dublin accent. He was as spit and polished as his bus. "Hop in, I'll get the luggage, and we'll pick up a lady from your group at the airport. Then we're off west to Bunratty near Shannon, where we'll be meetin' the rest of the folks."

Climbing aboard and sinking into the comfy front seat, I was overjoyed to find the bus as gorgeous inside as out. Everyone would have a great view with plenty of space to spread out and, if they wanted, to sit quietly by themselves. A tour to sacred sites can evoke joy or sorrow, pleasure or discomfort, as powerful energies are stirred. Individuals sign up for a spiritual tour, like this one, because they want to experience the unseen world and elementals specialize in creating situations to facilitate shifts in awareness. On that bright morn I was innocent of how many 'situations' were about to be hatched.

"Everyone will be so pleased," I thought, luxuriating in my good fortune as I watched the Irish countryside move by. My eyes savoured the emerald green of spring, a colour I've only ever seen in Ireland. The green so pulses with light and life that it's almost fluorescent. The blooming, yellow gorse and hawthorn called to me like the breath of my ancestors, and my heart opened, as it always does, when I return to Ireland. Here magic and the gates to other realms are still open. How I longed to share this with my fellow travellers.

I had about one hour of bliss before the first difficulty arose. We'd pulled into the parking area of the Dublin airport and waited for Diana, a friend since I was eighteen, to arrive. Helen left her seat and tried to open the toilet door. Finding it locked, she walked by me and approached Paddy.

"Paddy, could you unlock the door to the toilet?" she asked politely.

"I can't do that," he said. "It's locked."

"Could you unlock it?"

"No, don't have the key," he replied succinctly.

At this point, warning bells started to ring in my head, so I leaned forward to speak with Paddy. "When can you unlock it?"

"Can't," said he. "If you wanted to use the toilet, you would have had to request that before the tour."

"Oh my God!" I was thinking. "Thirty people on a bus for hours and no toilet. Okay, let's not panic. I'm sure it can be straightened out as soon as we meet Brian from Gallows Tours in Bunratty."

Helen and I shared a quick 'only-in-Ireland' look as she headed off to find a WC. Shortly thereafter, Diana's plane landed and, in the joy of seeing her, the toilet situation faded to the background. Diana is a self-confident, attractive woman with an infectious smile and kind eyes, behind which lurks an adventurous and restless spirit. There are some people who are shining stars and wayshowers to others and Diana is definitely one of these. I once suggested to her that she write a book on friendship because it would be hard to think of someone having more close friends than she. You could say it's her gift, one that has made her a skilled counsellor and trainer. People instinctively trust her. *geruandl, gesdriözv*

All of us had a lot to share because Molly, Helen, and Diana were students of mine from Canada and had known one another for several years. They loved elementals and, like the others who were joining us, sought spiritual experiences with them at the sacred sites we would visit. They also, like most of the other tour participants, hoped for a fun vacation. Not too much to ask—one would hope.

After several hours of driving and happy chatting we turned down a country lane and pulled into the driveway of a very nice bed-and-breakfast, just a few minutes' walk from Bunratty Castle. Several of the others had already arrived and were sitting bare-armed on benches, soaking up the sun—always a good idea whenever the weather permits in Ireland. *gepflegt*

A tall, dark-haired, well-groomed, professional-looking man in his forties greeted me, as I disembarked from the bus. "Hi, I'm Brian," he said smiling and extending his hand, "from Gallows Tours."

"Great to meet you," I replied, shaking his hand before adding. "If we could, I'd like to go over the itinerary with you, Paddy, and your guide Michael, before the tour starts." *Reise route*

"Sorry, I'm off to pick up more people at Shannon airport, so you'll need to do it without me." Brian turned on his heels and hopped in his van, leaving me to get the people checked into their rooms. Michael was not around, so I left a message on his door requesting a meeting in an hour to go over the itinerary with him and Paddy.

An hour later, slightly anxious—it must have been a premonition—I entered a cosy parlour replete with old wood furniture laden with family knick-knacks. A warm, jolly giant of a man, just settling into middle age, arose from a comfy couch.

"Hello and welcome," he said, receiving my tiny hand in his broad one. "I'm Michael, your guide." Michael wore a baggy extra-large T-shirt over a rounded tummy that spoke of serious love of food and no desire for exercise. Whereas Paddy and Brian were spick and span like new pennies, Michael looked as if he'd slept in his clothes.

A moment later, Paddy walked through the door and the three of us sank into well-stuffed chairs to peruse the itinerary or, to be more exact, 'itineraries', as, shocked, we discovered that each of us had a different version. Paddy had the original itinerary of the tour, the one that I had created with my Canadian tour company, which I had thought we were following. For the first time I examined the one that Gallows Tours had emailed me the day I departed Canada and realized that it bore little resemblance to my original agenda.

Stunned, I asked them, "How could this happen?"

"James only sent my itinerary last week and I don't even know where some of these sites are that you've planned," Michael said, no longer smiling. He finished off with, "and I've obviously not had time to do the research."

I'd seen Michael's résumé. Impressed that he had written at least twelve books about Irish folklore, including ones on faeries and leprechauns, I'd felt he would be a kindred spirit, a perfect guide for our *Mystical Tour of Ireland*. Imagine my surprise, therefore, to hear that he did not know many of the sites on our various itineraries. At that moment, I did not understand why Michael, who had devoted his entire life to studying elementals, had little interest in actually experiencing them firsthand. Only later, during the course of the tour, did I discover these reasons hidden behind his hail-fellow-well-met exterior.

Before I could deal with Michael's disclosure, Paddy chipped in. "Yes, and I've just found out that Brian's not seen to me lodging nor food for the whole trip. Now, that's just not right," he continued, raising his voice. "In fact, if this isn't sorted out immediately, I'm out of here with me bus."

After a year and a half of preparation, we were in the midst of a disaster. Adding my annoyance to theirs would solve nothing. So I spoke in what I hoped was a placating manner, "Paddy, I'll make sure your accommodation and food gets straightened out when Brian returns. For now, why don't we go over the itineraries and see what can be done."

Looking at our three versions we discovered that mine, having been sent just a few days prior, was the most recent, so we decided to follow it. Reviewing it, I discovered four out of my five requested accommodations had been changed. That was bad enough, but in examining the itinerary still further, I learned, to my horror, that one-half of the advertised sites—for which the participants had paid—had been dropped.

My idyllic tour was disappearing in the Irish mist. Ancient dolmens, healing wells, and sacred stone circles were no longer available. Instead, we were slated to visit Belfast and a deserted village. Somehow, I had to keep Paddy and Michael from bolting. I quickly decided to add a few other sacred sites in an attempt to rescue the tour before it fell over the cliff, and they both agreed.

As we were finishing up, Brian returned. Michael departed to ready himself for dinner leaving Brian, Paddy and me to sort out Paddy's accommodation.

"Just an oversight," assured Brian. "Don't worry, it will be taken care of."

"Phew," I relaxed. "One thing solved!" Taking a deep breath, I turned our attention to issue two. "We need to unlock the toilet on the bus. Is that possible?"

"No," said Paddy, vehemently. "I've already told you that, unless that's arranged before the tour, the door stays locked." Paddy was a 'by the book' kind of guy and anything, outside of what he expected, threw him off. Poor man. What the leprechauns could do with him . . . .

Looking at Brian, I waited to see what he would do. "Well, there's nothing I can do," he responded, shrugging his shoulders in a that's-just-how-it-is manner. "Guess you should have told James that you wanted to use the toilet, and he could have seen to it. He's in charge of all the organizational details. I just look after the people when they arrive, and I wouldn't usually go with a group that has a guide, but as your company is so large we wanted to make sure everything goes well."

"How could I know that there wouldn't be a functioning toilet on a fifty-seater bus?" I replied, trying to keep my voice calm and probably not succeeding. "James did not give us that information." ("The Lep", I was thinking to myself.)

Raising his hands in a gesture of helplessness, he replied, "Well there's nothing we can do now. It will work out."

I came to hear those same words from Brian many times in the course of the tour. Only later did I discover why Brian supported Paddy in his refusal to let us use the toilet. Brian let it slip in passing—it's very Irish to hint but not say something directly—that Paddy owned the bus, and that was why he didn't want to get his pretty new baby dirty. Brian had to keep Paddy happy, or we'd literally have *gesduvating* [handwritten]

no bus. The Irish can be very secretive—hard to believe given their garrulous nature, but true. Irish play their cards close to their chest and you can never be sure what the true facts of a situation are… unless they choose to tell you for their own reasons, and in their own time. A quality, by the way, which is also very like my leprechaun pal!

"Anyway, it's time we left for dinner," Brian said, looking at his watch and running out the door, leaving Paddy and me to gather up our stuff and follow. *taumeln, winkeln* [handwritten]

During dinner I attempted to greet everyone to make all feel welcome; yet inwardly I reeled from the day's events. In my mind I tried to sort out my responsibility and that of Gallows. My big question was, what could I do—other than what I was doing—to correct the situation? How could I see the diamond in the coal?

Eureka!

The lights flashed on as I suddenly realized more was happening than what appeared on the surface. I had not thought, until that moment, of the deeper level of significance that stared me in the face. All thirty people had come on a 'mystical tour' to meet and experience elementals. How could I have forgotten that, as soon as elementals are invited, nothing will be business as usual? Topsy-turvy is their specialty. I now knew that the 'tour' would be more of a 'pilgrimage' with elementals. */selesand den Kopf zu Stellen* [handwritten]

No sooner had that thought arisen than I recalled The Rolling Stones song, "You can't always get what you want, but if you try sometimes, you will find that you get what you need."

Smiling to myself I reflected that, although I was not getting the tour that I wanted or, let's face it, thought I deserved, magic was afoot. Naively believing myself to be an old hand in dealing with the leprechaun, I had assumed that the tour would be an effortless joy and vacation for others and myself. Now I began to glimpse the great experience of the Craic that Lloyd had planned for us.

*verdient
Magie war im Spiel
im Gange* [handwritten]

CHAPTER TWO

ST. BRIGID'S holy well and a wee bit o' history

Peering out the window, as the dawn broke, I saw that the weather still held fair. "Fantastic," I thought, my spirits lifting. "I wonder if it's a positive sign from the elementals?" "Every day's a good day in Ireland," I heard over my shoulder and turned to see my leprechaun friend lounging on the chair with his hands folded across his ample belly. He was tall for a leprechaun and came up to my shoulder. His feet, shod in gigantic old-fashioned Irish clogs, dangled above the floor. He was dressed in a tight-fitting green jacket that ended at the waist, and long woollen socks that joined his brown pants, just below the knee. Perched on his head was a top hat. All in all, the perfect picture of a leprechaun dressed in a country style not seen in Ireland for a hundred years.

"So you've decided to join us," I said telepathically, while pretending an aggrieved manner. "Look at the mess we're in, and the tour hasn't even started."

"Ah, me friends and I are really happy that so many 'humans' (pronounced 'huuumans') have come to Ireland to meet and tour with us," replied the leprechaun, struggling to hold back a smile. "You

27

humans" (there was that word again) "need to lighten up, not take things so seriously, enjoy life, and we're going to help you do that. Anyway, it's time for breakfast. Let's go." He leapt off the chair and, winking at me, walked straight through the closed door.

I was the first to arrive in the breakfast room—or should I say the first 'human'—as you-know-who was already seated at a corner table. The kitchen door swung open; the lady of the house walked over to inform me that crepes were on the menu.

Now, a bit of history. My leprechaun friend likes—actually one step down from craves—a traditional Irish breakfast of porridge and tea. New-fangled modern food, like crepes, did not bode well for the leprechaun and, by extension, for our tour.

"Could I have two bowls of porridge as well?" I asked, as nicely as possible. Little did she know how much depended on her answer.

"Why two? There's just one of you," she replied, not pleased, and I could tell she had decided I was a pushy tourist. As soon as my pal heard her answer, he jumped to his feet in a huff and, throwing me an it-is-all-your-fault look, stomped out the door. It occurred to me that he too could use a lesson in "lightening up."

Breakfast over, I walked to the parlour for the group meeting. I could hardly wait to tell the participants of all the sacred sites that we were *not* going to see. Woo-hoo! To make matters worse, Brian was no help, as he was conveniently off to the next tour stop to make sure, in his words, "that all is lined up there."

"Well, I'm glad he's on the ball now," I thought optimistically. "At least we've got the tour back on track."

So many of us had gathered in the parlour that we spilled over into the dining room and hall. At least half of the folks had no chairs and were leaning on various walls and the shoulders of their companions. Our guide, Michael, scrunched in beside me, overlapping my chair, and the leprechaun was on my other side. Michael and I did the best we could to put a positive spin on the tour changes. Meanwhile, the leprechaun perused our folks over his bifocals, which kept sliding down his nose. Lloyd is no spring chicken, being over a hundred years old, middle-aged for an elemental, and beset by the same nearsightedness that affects so many aging humans.

The group accepted the changes more graciously than I had dared to hope. Many, like Diana, Helen, and Molly, were my friends or students or had been on a previous tour with me and trusted that all would work out well. What optimistic innocents we were that first day! All the better for the leprechaun and Craic to have their way with us.

Still under the illusion of being in control of our destiny, in order to better know our fellow travellers, each of us chose an angel card from a deck displaying positive words and images. These cards were our way of asking the universe the theme of our tour. The angel card drawn for the group was 'clarity,' and the one selected for my leprechaun friend was 'simplicity.'

"I guess that means for you to keep the lessons simple so we 'humans' can understand them," I nudged this thought to him.

"Don't you be worryin', Darlin'; it's a game lot of humans you've got here," he said, smiling mischievously while casting his eyes around the room, "and me and me mates have a great pilgrimage lined up to teach you the ways of the Craic."

I could not pursue the conversation, much as I would have liked to, as the pouch of angel cards had made their way to me. Dipping my hand into the pouch, I pulled out 'grace.' To me, grace has always been associated with the Holy Spirit, the feminine presence of the divine. Receiving the card 'grace' assured me that there would be *gifts* in everything that would occur on the tour.

"Your Christian idea of 'grace' is close to what we Irish call 'the Craic,'" said my friend in a professorial tone, looking at me over his bifocals. "It's where the magic and fun are in life, where you don't get what you planned, and you do get what you didn't plan."

"My Gawd," I joked, mimicking his Irish accent, "is that keepin' the lesson 'simple' for the poor human? I'm confused by yer meanin.'"

"You can't figure out the Craic in 'yoourr' mind," he replied grinning, as he attempted my Canadian accent. "The gift is in 'livingg' it, and we elementals are 'goingg' to take you on a great experience of Craic. In fact, we've lined up a tour of Craggaunowen to replace 'yoourr' cancelled Ulster History Park, so let's get the show on the road," he concluded, jumping to his feet and vanishing.

It took us 'humans' a bit longer to gather up our baggage, but soon we piled on the bus and drove the short distance to Craggaunowen. Disembarking, we were faced with a confused Michael—a guide, if you can imagine, with little to say! Racing to the entrance booth, I grabbed a bunch of German and English brochures—the Italians were out of luck—and we set out to guide ourselves around the site. It had been years since I'd visited Craggaunowen, and I was hoping against hope that it would be as interesting as I had remembered. Luckily, we were on a roll that day and grace was with us all the way.

Craggaunowen is a reconstruction of a *crannog*—an artificial island where people during the late Bronze and through the Iron Age (600 BCE to 400 CE*) built houses, kept animals, and lived in relative security. Homes of these early people were thatched and made of wattle and daub (mud). Craggaunowen also has a ring fort, which is an earthen bank and stonewalls surrounding a type of habitation and farmland community that was common throughout Ireland, even into the thirteenth century.

---

* BCE and CE, meaning before the common era and common era, are employed increasingly to replace the Christian designations of BC and AD. For ease of reading CE is implied and not used throughout the text.

Craggaunowen

The beauty of Craggaunowen is that we could see with our own eyes how the Irish had lived for thousands of years until modern times. At the time when these people lived in ring forts, there was such a high level of scholarship that, after Greek and Latin, Irish was the third written language of Europe. Not only did Irish monks and scholars keep civilization alive by travelling throughout Europe during the Dark Ages, but also they most probably sailed to America.

At Craggaunowen there is a reconstruction of a small—and I mean *small*—leather-hulled boat similar to that in which St. Brendan, who died in 583, was said to have discovered the 'Promised Land' across the Atlantic. This reconstruction was actually sailed from Ireland to North America, proving that the Irish might well have preceded Columbus and the Vikings by hundreds of years.

As I meandered along the forest path on my way back to the bus, I reflected on the genial warmth of the Irish people, which strikes anyone who has travelled to Ireland. However, if you stay longer and delve deeper, you discover another gift of the Irish—a rich mystical tradition that has infused Ireland from the dawn of history.

"That's absolutely true," Lloyd piped up, falling in beside me as I re-boarded the bus to set off for our next stop—St. Brigid's Holy Well.

"Still," he said, plopping down in the seat next to me as Paddy pulled out, "if yer gonna tell a story, you might as well get it exact-like," he added, beginning in the true form of a *seanchaí*, the Irish word for their traditional storytellers.

"In the early times that you see at Craggaunowen, there were more elementals than humans in Ireland. We both had our own cultures, although we cross-fertilized each other, if you know what I mean."

"Could you be more 'exact-like'?" I joked, picking up on his country phrasing.

"As I was sayin'," replied my pal haughtily, but not, I noticed, without a twinkle in his eye, "we elementals are way in advance of humans in music, storytellin', and poetry, and one of the reasons the Irish—humans that is—are so good at recitin' stories and poetry by heart is that we elementals taught 'em."

"So humans and elementals got on well in earlier times in Ireland," I commented.

"Not just in Ireland, humans and elementals originally had respect for each other's traditions and talents all over the world," the leprechaun added. "That changed, of course, with the comin' of technology; this is why elementals are said not to like iron. Silver, gold, and copper are our metals, but with iron came technology, and it's been a steep downhill for elementals ever since."

My chum spoke to me, not only in words, but also in telepathic images. His tale was accompanied by assorted elementals being crowded over a steep cliff by humans wielding computers and cell phones.

"Gawd, you're grumpy," I said jokingly, while sending a telepathic image of him getting no porridge for breakfast.

"Well, a lot of the early monks and nuns in Ireland weren't half bad," he said, relenting and trying to keep a grin off his face. "To be sure, I'm speakin' of the ones that honoured the Earth and the old traditions, and Brigid was one of 'em. Did you know that yer St. Brigid bore the name of Brighid, one of the most powerful goddesses of what you humans love to call the 'pagan' religion?"

"She even built a monastery for nuns and monks at Kildare in the fifth century at a location previously sacred to your 'pagan' goddess Brighid," I said, eager to make a link.

Lloyd cut in to make certain I understood the 'real' history. "Brighid's father, Dubhthach, was a pagan king of Leinster, and believed in us and the old ways, but her mother, Brocca, was unfortunately a Christian who had been baptized by *that* Patrick."

I was only too well aware that my leprechaun comrade was a supporter of Brigid, and not so keen on *'that'* Patrick, who had done his best to drive goddess and nature worship out of Ireland.

"The good news is that St. Brigid, along with St. Patrick, is a patron saint of Ireland and so the link to the mother goddess is kept alive here," I said to my friend in a conciliatory manner. "It is likely that, without Celtic Christians like Brigid, patriarchal Christianity would have wiped out all traces of the goddess and nature religions long before the twelfth century—as they did in the rest of Europe."

"That bein' as it is," he replied, rising from his seat, for he so loved to have the last word, "it's still time that humans regained a balance with elementals, the Earth, and natural law. I, for one, am up to helpin' that happen."

At that moment, we arrived at the grotto with St. Brigid's Holy Well and our lot disembarked from the bus. I joined Michael for his historical talk, which he gave with renewed confidence, as he knew lots of comfortable facts to draw on. I had only listened for a few minutes when I heard the leprechaun's voice.

"Could you bring the 'huuumans' over here and get them in a circle," he shouted in our direction.

Fortunately, Michael was just finishing; so I was able to point the 'humans' towards the entrance of the grotto, where the leprechaun stood, and suggested that they form his requested circle.

"Michael, you are welcome to join us," I invited, as the others departed.

"No, I'm all right," he replied, still smiling, with his arms across his chest. His meaning in Irish was clearly 'not on your life'. As guides on my other tours have always wanted to take part in the spiritual rituals, I was disappointed by Michael's reaction, not just for myself, but also for the communal feeling in our group. Yet, it was early days for this tour, and I had hopes that my elemental pal might still win him over.

Statue of St. Brigid at the Holy Well

Making my way toward the entrance of the sacred well, I was astounded to see the leprechaun holding a crook resembling the one held by the nearby statue of St. Brigid. It looked like a cross (no pun intended) between a shepherd's staff and a Bishop's crosier. An elaborate headdress, similar to the kind that a medieval Pope might wear while giving a special ceremony, had replaced the leprechaun's usual top hat.

In leprechaun hierarchy, the head leprechaun, who is equivalent to the Pope, is called 'The Grand'. Although I'd known for a long time that my friend was held in great esteem amongst his kin and other nature spirits, I had not realized, until that moment, that he was a high ranking spiritual leader of them. Leprechauns are renowned for their secrecy and, even after the years I'd known him, my pal often surprised me with new bits of information. Reflecting back on his last words on the bus, I now understood that Lloyd, as self-appointed elemental leader of our tour, was preparing his own ritual of healing for us.

"Give each 'human' a candle and ask him or her to remain silent," said the leprechaun to me, while pushing back his headgear, which was balanced precariously and threatened to fall off.

When everyone had a candle, the leprechaun pointed his crook at the entrance to the grotto and a light flared from within. He wanted to create a ritual of healing, both for Brigid's well and for our folks, and was employing the energies of the site to do this. A deep peace pervaded the grotto. Pictures of St. Brigid and Mother Mary rested on the rocks overhanging the spring, reinforcing the harmonious connection between 'pagan' nature goddess and Celtic Christianity. Silver and gold charms of arms and legs, coloured ribbons, and fading flowers left by penitents seeking healing could be glimpsed festooning the walls inside the entrance.

Witnessing the reverence with which our thirty men and women waited to enter fed my heart. Ranging in age from thirties until early seventies, we hailed from the US, Canada, Holland, Germany,

Switzerland, Italy, and Britain. Such a mixed group, externally, it would be hard to find, as older Europeans, dressed in conservative beige slacks and oxfords, stood beside younger Americans with blue streaked hair, garbed in flamboyant pastels. Yet, each held his or her candle silently; some with their eyes closed in prayer, some gazing at the entrance in contemplation.

When my turn came, I entered the grotto, lowered myself to my knees, and prayed for the Earth and all beings. Looking to my right, I noticed with surprise that the leprechaun also knelt. Humility is not his strong suit. I waited silently, until he was finished, and then together we left the grotto.

"What does this well mean to you?" I asked him gently in my mind.

Rousing from his inner contemplation, a state unusual in him, he responded, "There always have been healin' wells in Ireland goin' way back before Christianity. The waters are healin', as they're energized by streams of spirit energy running through the Earth."

"We 'humans' call those streams leylines, or dragon lines, and they run like a grid linking up acupuncture points around the Earth."

"That's the right of it," replied my friend exuberantly, his love of teaching returning. "As I was sayin', these streams of energy from spirit merge with nature, feedin' the whole Earth and all beings on it. At certain places the energy gets so strong that it bubbles to the surface makin' that water much stronger for healin' all manner of things. And the water here is some of the strongest in all of Ireland."

"Does it affect the healing force of the water whether pilgrims worship Mother Mary or St. Brigid here?" I asked.

"Actually, there are two schools of thought amongst elementals," he replied, in his best scholarly tone. "Just as there are fundamentalist humans, there are fundamentalist elementals. These folks think that their way is best, and they don't want to have no truck with others. Elemental fundamentalists don't like it that Christians have taken over their sacred springs. However, I don't agree with 'em, or I wouldn't be bringin' *our* pilgrimage here."

Overjoyed at his assertion of leadership of 'our' tour, the leprechaun doubled over with a belly laugh, accidentally dumping his Pope's hat on the ground. This only caused him to laugh more. Finally, gathering himself together with as much dignity as he could muster, he smiled at me and, with a wink, disappeared.

While people were gathering up their belongings, one of the group members, Carl, a well-known German doctor, approached me. A tall, lean man with longish white hair receding from the brow, attractive and fit despite his almost seventy years, Carl makes medicines gathered from healing waters from all over the world.

"This water in the well is very good. It has a very high vibration," Carl commented in his husky German accent, while holding his pendulum, notepad, and a vial of water. He told me how high, but I can't remember now as numbers never seem to stay with me. Carl, however, confirmed all the leprechaun had said.

"Why wouldn't he?" I heard Lloyd's voice in my head. "Dr. Carl and I are on great terms. He works with the elementals all the time."

That was the last I saw of my leprechaun friend that day. We continued on to the Cliffs of Moher and from there to Galway, a city famous for the best Irish music in Ireland. Sadly, we were lodged in the suburbs in at least five different guesthouses. The coordinator of the accommodation seemed a fast friend of Brian's. No more said. To their credit, our hosts offered to run us eager music lovers into town, and a couple of carloads took them up on the offer.

Diana, never one to pass up a chance at music, or any outing for that matter, Kirsten, a stunning tall blond with looks guaranteed to draw men's eyes, and I wandered the old narrow lanes of Galway seeking traditional Irish music. Walking by the centuries-old stone and wooden shopfronts, passing locals speaking Gaelic which the

Irish call Irish we entered the pub district. Strolling along, we met laughing university students emerging from one pub from which shocking disco and rap could be heard. The twenty-first-century 'musac' had infiltrated Galway.

Not to be defeated, we continued our quest and kept our eyes peeled for the oldest pub that we could find. Rounding a corner, Diana, always the first to spot the best deal in any situation, happened on a pub with an old wooden front and door darkened with age. Swinging the door open, she led the way into a large room stuffed to the gills with happy mortals all holding pints of various brews in their hands. Traditional tunes wafted through the air above the noisy din.

A traditional Irish pub is unlike those in North America. For a start, hardly anyone eats. It's not a restaurant; it's definitely a place for a pint or two and lots of conversation. Now, trying to get that pint is not always easy, as the masses, two or three deep, cluster around the central bar. But what an eye those bartenders have! They seem to be able to spot even the shortest customer—for whom I usually qualify—at the back of the cluster and call out, "What'll it be?" Oftentimes, when sound will not carry, they just point to a glass, and you point to the handle of the right beer on tap. Once the glass is filled, a path to the bar usually opens so you can pay. Strange how that happens!

Then, armed with a thick, dark Guinness or, in my case, a bitter shandy made of lemonade and bitter beer, you attempt to hold the glass steady while people, running the gauntlet to the loo, bar, or door, continually jostle you from all sides. Tiny stools around even tinier tables are found lining the walls, but never imagine that one will be free. Why get your hopes up? Instead, your best plan is to try to stand as close to the music as possible. You will never be able to locate the musicians by sight and will have to follow your ear to find them. They are not on a stage as they would be in North America;

they are seated in a corner somewhere. The Irish usually ignore the entertainers because, as I've said, they're at the pub for a pint and to socialize. However, follow the other tourists and you'll find them crowding around the musicians. Kirsten had more than a few inches on Diana and me, so when she spotted the musicians she went forth armed with a dazzling smile and the admiring men made way for the sun. We followed closely in her wake.

That night in Galway three musicians were playing guitar, flute, and the Irish hand drum called the *bodhran*, pronounced 'bowrun.' Now, I have terrific fantasies about playing the *bodhran*, so I couldn't keep my eyes off the young woman who was doing just that. It's often difficult in Ireland to tell professionals from amateurs, as so many Irish play for fun. These three were fairly good and, typical of Irish musicians, they spoke infrequently to the audience, and then only to introduce the songs. They spent their time playing.

Enjoyable as the pub and music were, our wee party packed it in before eleven, which is 'last call' in a pub that holds to regulations and an early night by Irish standards. It had been a long day and we had to be well rested in the morning to ascend the mountain Croagh Patrick. Lying in my bed before sleep, I reviewed the day and a feeling of gratitude rose in me for all I had been given—Craggaunowen, St. Brigid's Well, great music and a bitter shandy at the pub, super company to travel with…and my leprechaun pal Lloyd. All perfect gifts of grace.

"Don't forget to thank the Craic," I could hear my leprechaun friend congratulating himself, as he slipped the final word into my thoughts.

chapter three

climbing croagh patrick

"ime to get up," I heard the leprechaun's cheery voice. Half opening my eyes, I saw him standing over me, wearing a backpack and leaning on a hiking stick. He had not surrendered his top hat or Irish clogs, so he was quite a picture.

"I would have thought that the last place you'd want to go would be one devoted to St. Patrick. Wouldn't you say he was the enemy?" I inquired, yawning. Elementals, I reckoned, would vote for pagans, who respected them, over Christians any day.

"The whole point, me dear girl," he said, humouring me, "is that we're takin' back the mountain today. The Reek (the local name for Croagh Patrick) is the highest mountain in Ireland and long before Patrick came it was the home of the sky gods. We called it *Cruchan Aigli* in Irish, meaning Eagle Mountain, and sure it's been a pilgrimage site for more than the 1500 years that yer humans credit. Even yer history says that there was a ring fort at the summit of our mountain prior to the Christians, and they've found megalithic tombs, standing stones, and burial sites around The Reek. It's not just for Christians, The Reek is for elementals and pagans too. So up you get, and let's hope there's some decent porridge."

With those words, he meandered slowly to the door, made a great show of opening it and, mocking the effort it takes for humans, put one foot laboriously in front of the other as he walked through the doorway. Smiling at his antics, I quickly gathered my hiking gear together and went to breakfast. On the sideboard were fruit, juice, corn flakes, but guess what—no porridge. Just then our hostess entered.

"Could I have two bowls of porridge please?" I asked, quickly adding in an attempt at fairness, "If I don't have any bacon and sausage with my eggs." Actually, I haven't eaten pork for over two decades, so my compromise caused me no pain whatsoever.

Peggy, a tall, athletic member of our assembly, dressed in a multi-pocketed beige hiking vest, was eating nearby. Overhearing our conversation, and knowing why I was asking for two bowls of porridge, she quickly piped up, "He can have mine."

Our hostess gave us a strange look, as there was no 'he' in the room, but returned a few minutes later with two heaping bowls of porridge. She put both of them down in front of me and, as innocuously as possible, I moved one of the bowls to the 'seemingly' empty seat to my right.

My leprechaun friend picked up a big spoon—no little ones for him—and started into the porridge. "Real porridge, rich and creamy," he said in a muffled voice between bites. "Not that instant stuff in a package that they're tryin' to pass off as porridge these days."

I must say I agreed with my friend as I'm not keen on that 'instant stuff' either.

"Yer friend there," he slurred, pointing his heaped spoon in Peggy's direction. "She's going to have a great experience on the mountain today."

My eyes tracked over to a bespectacled Peggy who was head-down shyly eating her porridge by herself.

"Does that have anything to do with the fact that Peggy got you some porridge?" I asked, amused and knowing it had.

"Thems that help us, we help," replied my pal. "You know that.

That's the pot o' gold we leprechauns gift to those who respect and aid us. Sure enuf, sometimes it's money we give folks. But, more of the time, our pot o' gold is bringin' magic and opportunities into yer life, so that you humans grow into the best you can be. All with a wee bit o' fun too, don't forget that."

"And do you think I could have a little help with the pilgrimage running smoothly today?" I charmed, trying to take advantage of his happy porridge-fed mood.

"Oh, we'll be givin' everyone LOTS of help today," replied Lloyd, finishing his breakfast and standing up. "See you on the mountain."

After his departure, I suddenly remembered that he had been non-committal about helping our day to run smoothly. I've learned, over the years, that the leprechauns' omissions in speech often mean that the magic of the Craic is only a few heartbeats away.

Sometime later, after most of our people had eaten, our hostess came to gather up the dishes. "Where are you off to today?" she asked.

"We're going to climb Croagh Patrick," Marion, who looked to be one of our less fit pilgrims, replied happily.

A heavy pause ensued before our hostess volunteered, "Oh, I did that on my honeymoon and it was terrible. I barely made it, and I'll never do that again."

Obviously, it was high time for the leader to gather more facts. "My guidebook said that the walk up Croagh Patrick takes two hours, and it can be done in one hour if you walk fast," I said, attempting to keep my voice calm for the others.

"Oh no," she replied, shaking her head sceptically. "It's four or five hours up and down; that's if yer fit. I wouldn't be goin' up, if I wasn't fit," she added, gazing meaningfully at Marion who was carrying more than a few extra pounds. I had met Marion, a huggable middle-aged woman from the States, for the first time the previous day. She had come on the tour because she loved my book and wanted an experience with elementals. Given what we were now hearing from our hostess, I only hoped that Marion would be okay on the walk.

"Good Lord," I was thinking to myself, with more than a dash of self-pity. "Is anything going to go as easily as planned?" Neither my Canadian travel company nor Gallows had told me that there was any difficulty walking up the mountain, or that it would take longer than the two hours I'd put on the brochure.

While folks were loading on the bus, I asked Paddy, Michael, and Brian, who were clustered together, if they'd ever done the climb. "No, I have not," was the unanimous response, but Michael had heard it would take about four hours.

"Will any of you be going with us today?" I asked hopefully.

"We will not," all three replied in tandem. I was shocked that Gallows had no guide to accompany us, if for no other reason than safety, and it was becoming increasingly clear that none of them had any personal interest in exploring spiritual sites. The tour was strictly business for them. Although I could understand Paddy's point of view as a bus driver, and Brian's as a tour organizer, I was amazed at Michael, whose work was devoted to writing and teaching about elementals and spiritual topics.

"Twenty-five thousand Christian pilgrims climb the mountain every July, and barefoot if they can, so how difficult could it be?" I thought, trying to put my anxiety at rest. The closer we drove, the larger Croagh Patrick loomed above us. Not a good sign. I was not alone with my concern, as more than a few of us had heard reports at the bed-and-breakfasts of a strenuous climb. Therefore, I was relieved, when we arrived at our starting place, to spot a man selling pilgrimage walking sticks.

Going straight to his stand, I came directly to the critical points: "How long and how difficult is the walk?" I asked.

"Ah, it will be four hours anyway," he replied, scanning our men and women to assess their fitness level.

"How hard is it?" I inquired a second time, wanting to make absolutely sure I had as much information as possible.

"I climb it all the time."

He was in his late fifties or early sixties, so I relaxed with his words. I should have remembered that Irish and North American levels of fitness are different, as the Irish, in general, have a more physically active lifestyle with more walking and working on the land, especially those living in rural areas.

By now, some of our pilgrims had decided not to climb the 765 metres to the summit. I was relieved that they, given the most comprehensive information, were making safe decisions. Even if folks didn't climb, I wanted everyone to experience the power of the mountain as fully as possible, so I requested that we all form a circle. As we gathered together, air elementals joined us causing the wind to increase in force.

Good old Lloyd watched us from the periphery. He was accompanied by many elementals, both large and small, all dressed in hiking gear. Tall, solemn male and female elves looked like an ad from a high-class fashion magazine, while knee-high gnomes and brownies outdid each other in brilliant colours guaranteed to wake up anyone gifted with second sight. Two young trolls stood barefoot, leaning on oversized hiking poles made from sapling trees. Meanwhile, a stocky leprechaun in a tight-fitting green-and-red jacket was helping his female companion in a long brown skirt to adjust her pack. Beside them, a long-nosed goblin in oversized hiking boots was fidgeting in a failed effort to stand still, his eyes darting here and there, possibly looking for mischief.

All of them, following Lloyd's lead, moved together to make an outer circle around us. There being as many elementals as humans, it dawned on me that each elemental intended to partner a human on the pilgrimage. My leprechaun friend and I have worked for many years to bring elementals and humans together to heal the Earth and here it was happening. My eyes grew teary at the sight.

Croagh Patrick has been a Christian pilgrimage site for hundreds of years. St. Patrick, along with St. Brigid, is the patron saint of Ireland, and he is said to have fasted for forty days on the summit of the mountain in 441 and to have built a church there. Ruins of a church at the summit have been dated at approximately 432 by radio carbon dating, which supports this oral history.

At the end of his forty-day fast, St. Patrick supposedly battled with the queen of the serpents and banished all the snakes from Ireland. As snakes have not been in Ireland since the last Ice Age, the snakes he banished were symbolic of the druids, and of the earlier goddess-based religion, both of which considered the snake to be sacred. Because snakes shed their skin annually, they are a symbol of death, rebirth, and transformation for nature-based religions.

It is likely that the main reason St. Patrick went specifically to The Reek was because the druids had celebrated the pagan ceremony of *Lughnasa*, named after the Tuatha De Danann's sun god Lugh, at its summit. The Christian pilgrimage, in fact, takes place the last Sunday of July, coinciding with the ancient harvest festival of Lughnasa.

You might go on pilgrimage to Ireland and never encounter St. Brigid, but it would be impossible not to run into St. Patrick. Unfortunately for the leprechaun and his elemental friends, St. Patrick was only too successful in Christianizing 'pagan' Ireland. Although St. Patrick was not the first missionary from Britain to Ireland, he had the greatest impact. It's not certain if Patrick was a monk himself, however, he established many monasteries throughout Ireland before dying in 493 at over a hundred years of age.

Addressing both humans and elementals, I began, "Just as Pope Paul asked for forgiveness for the atrocities that the Catholic Church has perpetrated in history, we humans must ask for forgiveness for what we have done to the Earth, to elementals, and to our physical bodies."

The elves and a few of the older leprechauns gazed on solemnly, while the goblins and gnomes, with nods of approval, clapped their hands on the backs of their fellows. My leprechaun friend leaned on his walking stick and smiled at me indulgently, as a teacher would a good student.

Addressing the humans, I continued, "The goal is not just to reach the summit, but to find your own pace, and to walk the amount that your body wants. Some of you might only walk for ten minutes and then sit in contemplation. Others might feel drawn to complete the walk and, if so, do this for others who either cannot, or prefer not, to go to the top. It is important to realize our interdependence."

I lit sage to purify us, and elementals squeezed into the gaps between the humans so they could get smoked as well. The goblins wheezed and grabbed their throats in mock horror of strangulation, and many gnomes and brownies turned green, even while pretending that they were okay. Meanwhile, the lean elves stood back and took the smoke in their stride with grace and dignity. The two young trolls, behaving like human teenagers, inhaled the smoke and blew rings, challenging each other to do better.

Croagh Patrick

With the purification ritual completed, the humans picked up their walking sticks, packed lunches and water, and began their ascent in silence. Diana, true to the athletic Greek goddess that was her namesake, led the pack. I watched the elementals, curious to see whom they would accompany and my leprechaun friend, on his best behaviour, joined me.

Dr. Carl was joined by an equally tall elf with a similar scholarly demeanour. Unsurprisingly, Kirsten's companion was an attractive female elf in flowing garb, probably a princess in the elemental realm. Molly seemed to have attracted a waist-high, long-limbed goblin with reddish eyes, hooked nose, and gnarled hands who was busy popping in and out of visibility. Goblins are usually the bad boys of the elemental world, therefore, I was astounded that one wanted to accompany a human. Peggy was ascending at a good clip, attended by a helpful looking female brownie garbed in oversized glasses and hiking vest that matched Peggy's own. The small brownie came only to Peggy's thigh, and was head-down, pumping her arms and trying unsuccessfully to match Peggy's long strides.

There were some unlikely combinations that only the elementals would understand. Especially interesting was one couple, Ute and Wolfgang, who had devoted their lives to developing healing medicines from plants. They were accompanied by many elementals including brownies, gnomes, and small flower faeries—all striving to be closer to them. Ute, a victim of too many years of overwork helping others, was not in the best physical shape and experienced difficulty walking. The elementals, knowing this, were only too happy to lend her a hand, as was Wolfgang, fit from many years of gathering plants in the wild, who stayed close by her side.

During the first hour, Ute, Wolfgang, Dr. Carl, and at least half of the pilgrims stopped and sought a quiet place to continue their silent contemplation. I walked briskly to check on people along the way and to make sure everyone was all right. I passed Marion, who was breathing heavily, as she continued slowly making her way up the mountain. The two teenage trolls were jostling each other for the honour of helping her.

Trolls have often received a bad rap in faery stories, eating people and such like, but I've found them helpful in a glum way. They are certainly the musclemen among elementals and the ones helping Marion were no exception. Although probably only twelve or thirteen in human years, Marion's trolls were broad with arms hanging almost to the ground. Their gigantic bare feet and hands were out of proportion to the rest of their body, and they were covered in excess hair by human standards. I had no doubt that either one of them could pick up Marion, not a small woman, and carry her off if they'd a mind to. Instead, they were patiently keeping her pace and trudging along slowly.

After two hours, the climb had become arduous and Diana, who was out in front, halted, turned around, and started back down. Diana works out at the gym daily, and we have done week-long hikes together; so I knew first-hand how fit she is.

"My Gawd," I thought to myself, "if Diana can't do it, there's no hope for me, or for many of us, to make it to the top."

She must have noted my concern because, as she reached me, she broke her silence to volunteer, "It's very difficult with the loose rock and I just realized that I didn't need to prove anything by summitting."

She had discovered the real meaning of listening to her body and respecting it and had made a decision that ran counter to her ordinary way.

My choice was different as I felt I was walking, not only for myself, but also for all those who could not do it. I often slipped on loose rock and sometimes had to use both hands to hold on. I was at the point of stopping when several young men in bare feet, delicate and vulnerable compared to the trolls, came around a corner just above me. You could see that they were celebrating a rite of passage into manhood by doing the walk the same way that pilgrims had done it for hundreds of years. I felt privileged to witness their struggle and, breaking my silence, greeted them with a bracing, "Good on you," before inquiring wearily, "How much further is it?"

"You are almost there, just another twenty minutes or so," one of the young men replied smiling, obviously proud of his achievement that day.

Gaining hope at his words, I decided to persevere and shortly thereafter arrived at the summit. Although the day was cloudy, the view over the ocean was still breathtaking. From there, you could feel the long history of the millions of people who had walked this pilgrimage up Croagh Patrick. Each had come for a different reason, perhaps to grieve a loss of a loved one, to pray for the touch of the Holy Spirit, to ask for a new job, or to receive a physical healing. For me, my silent walk had been in gratitude that my body, although no longer in the bloom of youth, could still enjoy hikes and pilgrimages. How fortunate I was to have such a healthy strong body when so many did not!

The wind was fierce at the summit, and it felt as if the air elementals were 'takin' back the mountain,' as my leprechaun friend had suggested earlier that morning. As more of our pilgrims arrived, so did their accompanying elementals. Lloyd gathered these elves, brownies, trolls, gnomes, and even the goblin who had been with Molly, off by themselves, to what end I cannot say with certainty. However, as The Reek was an ancient pilgrimage site for the Tuatha Dé Danann, who are ancestors of the elementals, I suspected the gathering had something to do with them. I sent my attention towards the elementals, but none of them would meet my glance, and I felt an invisible wall across which I should not pass.

All the elementals had made it to the top. Unlike humans,

elementals can travel in space and time just by thinking about where they want to go. This means that elementals could think themselves at the summit and they would be there. They did not have to huff and puff and struggle; yet, they had chosen to partner their much slower human companions.

Recognizing the elementals' desire to be left alone, I slowly started the descent. It turned out to be even more difficult than the ascent. Peggy, who was in excellent physical shape, passed me on the way down. I was astounded at her speed until, without warning, I witnessed her fall and hit her head on a rock. Praying she was unhurt, I hurried to her side. By the time I arrived she was sitting up with a big bump forming on her temple.

"I guess I wasn't paying attention," Peggy said, putting her hand over the wound.

"Are you all right?" I asked, gently examining her injury, worried about how serious head injuries could be.

Straightening her glasses and hiking vest and shuffling to her feet, she laughed off my concern. "I'll be fine, although I think I'll walk a little slower."

I was almost certain that Peggy's fall was what the leprechaun had been referring to at breakfast as a 'gift' from the elementals, although to be fair, I did not see any elementals near her. In fact, her friendly little brownie was probably still attending the conclave at the summit and, as brownies are the most helpful of all elementals to humans, she was unlikely to have done such mischief. Because elementals can see the future, my leprechaun friend could see what would happen to Peggy.

Also, if elementals take an interest in you, they might nudge you into a needed healing. Elementals are spirit's gardeners in the natural world, pruning us here and there to make us more beautiful and strong. Their function is to correct imbalances that they perceive in all living things. Their gifts often come in strange packages; the learning may occur in retrospect, and not in the present moment.

One of the wonderful things about the majority of people whom I've had the good fortune to be with on tours and pilgrimages is their generous and positive nature. Peggy was no exception. She did not complain about her injury, and together we continued our descent more slowly.

"I'm from the mid-western United States and have never travelled abroad before," she chatted pleasantly, shortening her stride to match my smaller steps.

"What a way to start," I thought to myself, while at the same time asking, "What brought you on this tour?"

"Lots of reasons. One was to travel with my sister Melanie and another reason was to meet you. But this is all new to me, elementals and stuff, as I think of myself as a Christian."

Peggy's openness, trust, and even courage in leaving her traditional background to try our group's non-traditional approach to spirituality touched my heart. About a half-hour from the bottom of the mountain, Peggy went on, while I waited to make sure that everyone made it back safely.

Many of the folks stopped for a few minutes to tell me how they had felt the elementals walking with them, and some had even seen them with their second-sight. This pilgrimage up Croagh Patrick had been deeply moving for many, but it was not yet over. An hour later, when two women still had not returned, I went to the bus to consult on what to do. By now the pilgrimage had taken more than five hours and some people, understandably, were tired of waiting and ready for their dinner.

Unfortunately, we couldn't depart before those last two women, Caitlin and Marion, arrived. Just at that moment, Caitlin, blue-streaked hair flying and intense almond-shaped eyes broadcasting alarm, climbed onto the bus. "Marion is still a good way back and a man is assisting her, but she's very tired," she gasped, breathless.

Even having two teenage trolls to help had not been enough for Marion. It now had to be humans to the rescue. Our guide, Michael, was not stirring himself, nor was Paddy, so I got to my feet, followed immediately by Diana and Max. Diana luckily was fit and rested, as she had not done the whole climb, and Max, whom I'd known from two previous tours, was always willing to assist anyone in need.

Max is a complex man and the fifth husband of Melanie, Peggy's sister. An internationally recognized art appraiser living in Santa Fe, New Mexico, Max is a practical guy who would normally not be drawn to a spiritual tour. Actually, I don't think he even believed in elementals, but he loved the history and culture of Ireland and listened to Michael's historical chats with lots of questions, eager to share what he had read. Max, unlike Diana, was not a physical type and had only walked a little that day. Yet, he had a big heart and wanted to rescue Marion.

I was grateful to both Diana and Max, for I was pooped. The others started on packages of cookies, crisps, or whatever was available to stave off hunger. Happily, Marion was closer than we had expected, and soon we saw her being helped by a man around the last bend of the trail. Her teenage troll companions still accompanied her, although their darting eyes and hesitant steps betrayed their nervousness about getting too close to the bus and civilization. It was eight pm before we had Marion safely back on the bus, where she was greeted by cheers from her fellow walkers.

In contrast, Michael and Paddy's silence and tense body postures conveyed their displeasure. Obviously, the tour was not going the way they thought it should. Turning the key in the ignition, Paddy jerked the bus into first gear and headed for the village of Keel on Achill Island, where we'd be staying for the next few days.

"Now wasn't that a great day?" Lloyd said, easing himself into the seat beside me.

Not waiting for me to respond, he glanced down at his feet that had steam rising off them and continued, "But me feet sure are tired. I don't know how you humans do all that walkin'. Still, it was needed if we were to take back the mountain from Patrick. It's on one of 'em energy lines that you were talkin' about yesterday."

"Do you mean that Croagh Patrick isn't Christian anymore?" I asked, puzzled at his words.

"Well, not exactly," explained my friend patiently. "Let's just say that yer friends and mine did a wee bit of rebalancin' the energy to be more fair both to humans and elementals. You can see how much better yer friends are for it," he commented, turning around in his seat to look.

It's true, I thought, as I gazed at the folks. Although Ute, Marion, Caitlin, and others had their eyes closed for a well-needed snooze, I observed that their overall energy was much higher than it had been before their day outside.

"How exactly did you rebalance the energy today?" I asked, eager to understand his point of view.

"One of the ways was by walkin' together and by lettin' bygones be bygones, between you humans and us. Seein' how hard it was for humans to walk kind of developed our sympathy, if you know what I mean? You might say you are handicapped-like, next to us elementals who can go wherever we want just by thinkin' about it."

"It's been a wonderful lesson today," I agreed, "about what we learn in going beyond our limits, either physically like Marion, or spiritually like Peggy. Sometimes life doesn't offer us a safety net— like no information or help," I said, nodding in Michael's direction. "Still, when we commit to trying something new, as we did today, our energy increases."

"If you keep yer thoughts positive, you don't get stuck in guilts and worries and yer energy increases," our wise friend added, wanting the last word.

"I'm curious to know what you elementals were doing at the top of the mountain?" I asked, changing the subject away from humans and back to elementals.

"If we'd wanted you to know, you would have been invited," the leprechaun retorted. "Don't think you know everythin'. You are still what you are, while I'm Himself."

"What do you mean 'Himself?'" I asked, puzzled by the term.

"Each of the four traditional provinces of Ireland: Ulster, Connaught, Leinster, and Munster, had an elected king," the leprechaun replied, moving into his professorial voice. "We elementals still stick to these old ways and each of these provinces still has an elected leprechaun called 'Himself.' We uphold the old laws—the Brehon Laws you humans call them—which are based on what's good for the community, and not just what suits the individual that you humans regard as soooo important. Accordin' to our laws, it is necessary for humans to make reparation to elementals. Doin' yer prayers for forgiveness today, whilst you were goin' up the mountain, was a good way to start."

"It does my heart good that your elemental companions are forgiving humans for what we've done to the Earth, and that they partnered us today. Still...I have a question," I asked, changing the topic and trying to understand his role, "Are you saying that you're like a king to the elementals?"

"That I am, Lass," he replied. "And more than that, some would say," he mumbled to himself. Before I could clarify what he was whispering about, he added, "Anyway, I'd best go and get ready to welcome you and yer friends back at me home on Achill. We've got a few things to sort out." With those elusive words, Lloyd departed.

chapter four

Coming home to Achill

I was looking forward to returning to the little village of Keel on Achill Island. It was in an old cottage on the outskirts of this very village that I first met my leprechaun friend many years ago. He and his family had lived in the cottage for almost a hundred years, and I had stayed there for the summer. Since then, I've been back to Achill twice, including six years ago with another group. For me, it was always like coming home, and much of this feeling had to do with the Unicorn, the small, family-run inn where we would stay for the next two nights.

I'd come to know the owners of the Unicorn, as occasionally I'd treat myself to a dinner there when I was living in the cottage. I had a real soft spot for the daughter, Mary, who felt like a sister to me. It's strange how we meet people and our hearts open to them with a recognition that goes beyond this life. That's how I felt about Mary. Also, I was fond of Mary's mother, who was still working in the dining room when I'd first come to Keel, but who had since passed on. On my last trip, I had come to know Mary's husband, Sean, a wee bit and was looking forward to seeing him as well.

Mary and Sean would have our dinner ready when we arrived around nine-thirty, or half-nine as they say in the West Country, which was two and a half hours later than planned. Yes, that night we'd eat dinner just as the Irish did. Late, very late.

Brian had gone ahead to Keel and the Unicorn to make sure all would be ready for us when we arrived. We'd been driving a while when Paddy's cell phone rang; I could tell when he answered that Brian was calling. As the conversation continued, it was easy to pick up from Paddy's anxious voice and hunched back that he was not pleased with what he was hearing.

Ending the call, Paddy looked over his shoulder at me and said, "Brian doesn't think I'll be able to get me bus up the lane in Keel as its too big. We'll have to park it somewhere else and take other transport."

"What other transport?" I asked, none too happy about this latest turn of events. "Keel is a village of a couple hundred people. It's a half-hour drive to the nearest town where we'd find taxis. Have you ever been to Achill, Paddy?"

"No," he said. "Who'd want to go to Achill?" His statement was delivered in the self-righteous tone of a city-loving Dubliner.

Paddy loved his new bus. He didn't want to dirty it by using the toilet, and now he didn't want to scratch it by squeezing up a tiny lane made for horse and carts, not for fifty-seater modern buses. Don't get me wrong. Paddy was a great driver; he was just nervous when asked to go somewhere he'd never been before. I didn't think there would be a problem driving to the Unicorn, but I wondered if Paddy would trust the judgment of a Canadian woman over that of Brian, who was both his employer and an Irishman to boot, not to mention that Brian was actually at the site. It was risky for me to interfere, as I'm certainly not, and never likely to be, a bus driver.

"Paddy," I said out of desperation, for as sure as tootin' I couldn't see thirty of us dragging our bags for three hours or more along a country road in the dark. "I've seen buses the same size as ours travelling through Keel, so I know it can be done. The worst that can happen, if you can't pull in the lane beside the Unicorn, is that we'll need to walk about a hundred yards with our luggage."

"Yer sure now?"

"Yes, I'm sure," I replied, sounding as certain as I could be given the circumstances. "I lived in Keel for a summer and have stayed with a group at the Unicorn."

"All right, we'll try it," Paddy said, deciding to trust me.

I found myself exhausted, not just from the walk, but also from the constant unpredictable problems. Only two days in, and there had already been more difficulties than on any other tour I'd led in over twenty years. It began to dawn on me that Brian was trying to catch up for the lack of planning by that elusive James the Lep. This resulted in Paddy and Michael's unpreparedness, and in putting a strain on all of us.

"I told you we'd sort it out," I heard the leprechaun's voice in my mind and realized that the bus incident was what he had been alluding to earlier. "Don't you go blamin' James. He's helped us with the Craic and, if it weren't for him, we'd only have half the magic to work with. You've got to trust me as Paddy trusted you just now. What's the sense of havin' a pilgrimage when you know everythin' that will happen ahead of time? There'd be no learnin' and no fun in it. That's why humans lose yer joy and we're givin' the fun of the Craic back to you—like a magic transfusion. If Marion had known it would take eight hours, she would never have climbed The Reek; and just look at her, ain't she pleased with herself?"

Turning around, I caught Marion's eye as a contented self-satisfied grin flooded her face. Lloyd was right, once again. Despite his unorthodox methods by human standards, you had to admit he certainly was transforming folks.

"Welcome back," he continued as we crossed into Achill.

The name Achill Island is misleading, as it is no longer an island, and you drive onto Achill right from the mainland near Mulranny.

The topography changes almost immediately upon crossing the bridge at Achill Sound. Wide-open, rugged land replaces the massive wild rhododendrons that lined the road earlier. Hills become higher, with fewer trees and, from time to time, one-storied bungalows, from which peat smoke sreams, dot the remote landscape. These simple squat homes are built close to the ground to cut down the force of the wind that continually gusts on Achill. About thirty minutes later, you see the village of Keel in the distance, sitting at the head of a bay surrounded by high cliffs.

My heart rose to my throat; it's always the same when I return to Keel. The magic of Ireland is still alive in the West Country, and I could feel it even from the bus. There's an openness and yearning in the country that beckons to the mystic in people. The veil between this and the other world is thin because in Achill elementals still reside alongside humans.

Most of our weary folks were awake by now and happy cries of "Look over there!" and oohs and ahs were heard throughout the bus. Fortunately, Paddy was able to drive right up the lane—proving there is a God—where Mary and Sean awaited our arrival.

"You're welcome," Mary greeted me with a hug as we dragged our exhausted bodies through the doorway. I hadn't seen her for several years, but even in middle age she retained the dark hair, freckled fair skin, and violet-blue eyes of an Irish beauty.

"I'm so sorry we're late," I said. "Croagh Patrick took hours longer than we thought."

"Not to worry. Yer here now and we've got a nice meal waiting for you. What's say, we do it in half-an-hour at ten? That will give everyone a chance to get into the rooms and wash up."

"Perfect," I said, overjoyed at being taken care of. I always felt at home with Mary. "Can I hand out keys and help our folks into their rooms?"

"Certainly," she accepted, smiling and, working as a team, we got the tired pilgrims settled in short order.

Mary put me in a lovely room overlooking the bay. The light still lingered and, gazing at the splendid view, I took a moment to soak up my good fortune at returning and bringing others to enjoy Achill's magic. After a quick wash and change of clothes, I strolled down the long, low-ceilinged corridors to the dining room. It was just as I had remembered it: cosy, with sunny yellow walls and lots of windows overlooking the garden and sea. The tables were set as beautifully as you would find in a five-star restaurant. Our starving folks arrived a few minutes later, all happy with their rooms, and Achill.

Because it was so late, the serving staff had gone for the day leaving an overwhelmed Sean attempting to serve thirty-plus ravenous people. Melanie, makeup perfect and dressed immaculately in current Santa Fe style, jumped to her feet from beside her husband Max. Rushing to the kitchen, she soon emerged carrying plates loaded with food, her glistening red-polished nails clutching the plates securely. Although she looked like a queen and preferred a classy joint to a tent any day of the week, Melanie, like her husband Max and sister Peggy, was always quick to assist where help was needed.

Mary is a fantastic chef and the dinner was delicious, with heaped helpings of boiled potatoes and carrots that are Ireland's common eating fare. The Irish would never hear of eating just one potato and would be insulted to be served such a measly amount. Best count on eating three or four if you're in Ireland.

In Craggaunowen I had bought some mead to share with the group for this very moment. Mead is a traditional wine made from honey, that, in ancient times, was drunk at weddings and other special events. It resembles a sweet sherry, but smoother and with a golden colour. I, like the elementals, am a big fan of it, and my leprechaun friend enjoyed it as well as Guinness. As soon as I started pouring the mead, the elementals appeared. Seeing this, I quickly invited the humans, if they so chose, to share their mead with the elementals. Many decided to do this and tried the mead first, leaving the remainder for their elemental friends.

If you were clairvoyant, you would observe that the elementals drinking the mead actually take the essence out of it, so that the mead no longer contains energy. Without clairvoyant vision, the glass of mead on the table looks the same as it did before. If a human drinks the mead, after the elementals absorb its essence, there is no nutrition in the food and it is like eating a waste product. This is much frowned upon by the elementals. That said, if you ever get on an elemental's bad side, it might insult you by taking the goodness out of your food, leaving you with the resulting garbage. Lest you think that elementals have been working at fast-food joints, let me assure you that they would not be caught dead in such a place. The food is already devoid of energy without any help from them.

"Don't stint!" commanded you-know-who, grabbing hold of the glass I was filling.

Looking around, I noticed the elementals gratefully accepting the mead. Peggy's brownie looked as if she'd had one gulp too many, and was holding her glass with both hands in an effort to not spill a drop on the tablecloth. The flower faeries, the very same who had accompanied Ute on Croagh Patrick, hovered over her glass taking sips that hardly made a dent in the energy. Molly's goblin, faster than all the other elementals combined, beat many of his fellows to the drinks offered by their human partners. The teenage trolls, observing this, decided to mimic the goblin and lumbered around the room trying to steal drinks, that is, until Dr. Carl's solemn elf intervened and scolded them. Seeing me notice him, the old elf nodded, gracefully acknowledging me. Telling the age of elementals is difficult, and especially so with elves, for they maintain their beauty even when old, but the eyes of the old elf held wisdom acquired most probably over many hundreds of years.

Hannah and Sara, two lovely women in their early seventies from Switzerland, sat quietly waiting for their glasses to be filled. They were both lifetime anthroposophists, as students of the twentieth century spiritual teacher Rudolf Steiner are called. Rudolf Steiner had met Lloyd almost a hundred years ago and had assisted him in forming a group of elementals to work with humans. I learned of this when I lived with Lloyd and his family in the cottage years before. Bringing together humans and elementals in partnership to help the Earth had been my leprechaun friend's main occupation ever since. Hannah and Sara, like Ute and Wolfgang and the other anthroposophists in the group, were interested in working more closely with elementals. This was their main reason for coming to Ireland.

"This mead is not for me, it's for the elementals," said grey-haired Hannah, smiling from her eyes down to her mouth, and extending her glass to be filled. Sara, taller and quieter than her gregarious friend, did the same. At that moment, twittering gnomes, about table-height, grabbed the glasses gratefully and downed the contents, saluting Hannah and Sara in the process. My leprechaun friend stood watching nearby. Catching my eye, he raised the glass I'd filled for him and, acknowledging me with a wink, finished the mead in one gulp.

"Those two ladies are special friends of ours," said my elemental pal. "They are always generous to us," he hinted, extending his empty glass to be refilled. "In fact, most anthroposophists believe in us and we've quite a followin' with 'em."

"I thought Rudolf Steiner recommended that people don't drink," I commented, holding the few remaining drops of mead close to my chest. "Hannah and Sara, as *proper* anthroposophists, abstain from alcohol."

"Well, there's rules; then there's *rules*," he responded, extending his arm still further. "The mead is goin' to fortify me for tomorrow, and I'll need it, bein' yer guide and all. Anyway, a drop is not hurtin' anyone. It just opens the door a little better for your humans to notice us."

With these words he took the almost empty bottle from my hand and, raising it in my direction, saluted my good health in pure Irish style. "*Sláinte,*" he said. "See you bright and early, and tell folks to wear good walkin' shoes." With that utterance, he vanished.

Confused by Lloyd's parting words about everyone walking, I went over to speak with Michael, Paddy, and Brian, who were eating by themselves in the next room. Looking up from his dinner, Brian began, "You'll have to walk tomorrow as you'll not have the bus. Paddy needs a day off every seven days; that's the legal regulation."

"What! We're only on day two," I thought, caught off guard.

Seeing my shocked look, Brian continued, "Paddy has to drive every day after we leave here, so we thought we'd give him a day off now."

It was fair, of course. It was just that, if I'd known earlier, I could have made other plans for our folks. I preferred to walk, but there were a few individuals, such as Hannah, Sara, and Ute, who would be very stretched to get to all the sites on foot. In fact, I doubted that some could do it. Nevertheless, I was starting to accept what I could not change and to embrace the magic of the Craic. My original idea that I was in charge of the tour was dissolving, as I, like my fellow pilgrims, became a participant in the leprechaun's pilgrimage.

"Remember to trust the Craic and meself, as much as you've always trusted yerself, and you'll be strikin' the right note," echoed the leprechaun's voice in my ear. "Sleep on that lesson tonight, me girl."

chapter five

The Leprechaun's Tour

U p you get!" I heard and, opening my eyes, I saw the leprechaun wearing his backpack, which had tripled in size from our pilgrimage the day before. He was trying unsuccessfully to open the heavy curtains. "Big day planned, big day planned," he muttered anxiously to himself, contending with the drapes.

Throwing off my covers, I walked to the window and, lending him a hand, drew back the curtains. "So what's the itinerary?" I asked cheerily, enjoying the morning light streaming in. It was a beautiful sunny day—so rare on Achill—and I knew we had the elementals to thank for their intervention.

Collapsing on the chair, he pulled a gigantic folder from his backpack on which was written in flowery script *Pilgrimage for Humans*. Breathing a huge sigh, Lloyd pushed back the old-fashioned bifocals that were resting on his nose.

"I've been up all night, while you were getting yer beauty rest," he said, glaring over the bifocals, "and I've got quite a day planned."

"Which is...?" I prompted.

"First, we'll go to Murchies to get a packed lunch, then we'll walk up the lane to me cottage, then on to the cemetery, next off to the dolmen, and finally back here for dinner. Do you have any more mead, by the way? I'll have earned it, don't you think, and we're goin' to have lots of help from all me friends." He winked with a mischievous grin, as he created an image of a gigantic bottle, with *Mead* written in bold letters, to appear on the table.

"Your plan sounds perfect," I responded, smiling at his antics. "I have no more mead, but I'll take you to the local for a pint when we're done."

"Done and agreed," he replied, replacing the image of the bottle of mead with an image of an equally gigantic glass filled to the brim with frothy Guinness. Making a big production of taking off the bifocals, he put them in a gaudy green case covered with shamrocks and tried stuffing the case and the copious notes back into his pack—without success.

The pages flew out of his hands and onto the floor. Instead of print, each page contained a fully coloured moving picture. I recognized the scene of very tired humans making the ascent of Croagh Patrick assisted by loving, helpful elves, and gnomes. This image captured what was obviously the leprechaun's perception.

Another page illustrated what could only be a future happening—that of happy humans and elementals gathered in a meadow amidst a crumbling building and being entertained by a tall, grey-bearded storyteller. I found it curious that many pages illustrated different versions of the same story and, from my point of view, some versions were definitely more desirable than others.

"Why is there more than one version of the same event?" I asked, wanting to understand how his system worked.

"It depends on the choices you humans make. How you react to certain things determines what happens to you next," Lloyd answered, as if explaining to a slow learner.

"Is there anything I could do to make the pilgrimage easier and more fun?"

"It's not so much what yer doin' or not doin'. There's thirty of you

and the Big Three"—an allusion to Paddy, Michael, and Brian—
"influencin' things and every single one of 'ems makin' choices.

"Give me back them pages, as yer not supposed to see 'em," my
friend demanded, wresting the pages from my hand.

Accompanied by more drawn-out sighs, the leprechaun put
his hand into the pack and pulled out wooden splints, bandages,
mysterious bottles with even more mysterious labels, and a gigantic
water bottle on which was written *Emergency Energy*.

"Are we going to need those?" I asked, alarmed at the articles.

"You never know," he said, in a laissez-faire tone, stuffing the
supplies back in his pack. "The goblins livin' on the lane want to be
part of the tour, and you can't include some and not others."

"The same goblins that don't like humans?" I asked, worried and
remembering my not-so-great-experiences with them when I lived in
Crumpaun Cottage.

"Sure enuf," Lloyd acknowledged. "But they're a 'little' improved,
if yer with me," he said with assurance. "Besides, it doesn't help that
an eejit is buildin' a posh monstrosity next to our cottage. It's not goin'
at all well for him. He's been at it for more than two years now and
it's still not finished. Can you imagine that?" the leprechaun laughed
mischievously.

"But the real thing is, the energy is a bit unpredictable today
and full of surprises. Not that I'm complainin', as it's a favourite
day for us elementals."

"Why is the energy unpredictable today?" I asked, trying to stay calm.

"It's Friday the thirteenth, don't you know?" the leprechaun
responded in good humour and, chortling with glee, disappeared.

Oh great! After all our harried folks had been through, my
elemental friend was going to use Friday the thirteenth to up the ante.
I resigned myself to yet more twists. The pilgrimage obviously had a
life of its own, and was not within the control of this one little human.

My best hope was to trust the process, as Lloyd had recommended the previous day. With that thought settling my mind, I dressed and went to breakfast.

A gigantic, delicious Irish breakfast awaited that included many versions of eggs, sausage, ham, bacon, home fries, and several kinds of toast. The homemade porridge was soaked from the night before and simmered slowly just the way my leprechaun chum prefers it. Ummm! Smooth and creamy, not heavy and gooey like the stuff amateurs make.

Peggy, Marion, and Caitlin, eager to get on the leprechaun's good side, set out porridge for him. Meanwhile, Peggy's little brownie, Marion's teenage trolls, and a small waist-high elf that was partnering pixyish Caitlin, hovered nearby. The sweet little brownie and elf appeared hung-over from the previous evening and were trying sips of the dreaded human addiction—coffee. The two trolls, definitely looking the worse for wear, were downing as many cups of coffee as they could get their gigantic hands on.

Finishing breakfast, we waddled to Murchies to buy sandwiches for lunch. "At least we've got food," I thought, amused at how low my standards had fallen for what made a good day. I had fond memories of Murchies from my summer in Keel. It was a family-run grocery store and post office, and I was pleased to see that it hadn't changed much from my days in the village. The only thing that had been added was a larger selection of sliced meats and rolls, obviously catering to the tourist trade, even though we were just about the only 'foreigners' around.

While people were buying sandwiches and sweets, I noticed elementals, some from the previous day and some new ones, gathering outside. Most were carrying backpacks. As with our hike up Croagh Patrick, there was an elemental for every human, with a few extra which, I had a hunch, were locals. Just as subtle clues allow you to tell a German from an Italian, so you can feel the difference between an Irish and an American elemental. We seemed to be forming our own United Nations that was as committed to peace amongst nations and races as our New York counterpart. Unfortunately, there were some young goblins milling about, poking each other, leering at the humans, and looking anything but friendly. Marion's young trolls and a few young leprechauns looked to be part of the goblin gang. Not a good sign.

Male and female elves, dressed with grace and style, stood off by themselves looking uncomfortable with the bad behaviour of the goblins. The elves did not appear to be locals, as some of the goblins were nudging each other and pointing towards them. I supposed that my leprechaun friend had invited assorted elementals from as many countries as there were humans. It was wonderful that the elementals were continuing their pilgrimage with us. However, it would have been nice if the leprechaun had informed me earlier of his intentions, as the more elementals there were, the more surprises and Craic we could expect. Knowing my friend, why would I be surprised?

He stood on the fringes of the elemental group, accompanied by a younger leprechaun about his size or—Heaven help my friend's pride!—a bit taller. Waving me over, my friend introduced me to the young leprechaun. "Seamus, this is Tanis," he said.

Seamus (pronounced 'Shamus' was not his real name, which I'm keeping private) looked shocked that his name had been given to me so lightly. Leprechauns never give their real names because you can control them, with the names, and call them whenever you want. My leprechaun friend had given me his real name, which is obviously not Lloyd, the summer I had lived at Crumpaun Cottage. He trusted me to keep it secret. So far, I've done just that.

"I'm happy to meet you and your name is safe with me," I said, addressing Seamus. Nodding toward my leprechaun pal, I asked

Seamus, "What's your relationship with this old codger?"

At my words a big smile broke out on Seamus' face. Before he could reply, Lloyd puffed himself up and, pretending his dignity had been hurt, cut in. "I've taken him under me wing and am showin' him the ropes."

As he spoke, a pair of fake angel wings descended onto my chum's shoulders and gigantic ropes, which would not have been out of place in a shipyard, appeared in a muddled pile at his feet. The leprechaun derives immense amusement from using human expressions and loves to show off his knowledge. He, like most well-developed elementals, can manifest visual images as easily as humans manifest words, and he loved teaching with these images.

"I'm studying with Lloyd the Grand," Seamus said, laughing as he emphasized the leprechaun's alias. I was amused to see that Lloyd had met his match in his young protégé.

"Let's get the show on the road," responded my pal, deliberately changing the topic. Mimicking a major-domo bandleader, he lifted his walking stick in the air and, catching the attention of the other elementals, headed out. Signalling to the humans, who had gathered by now, I followed in the leprechaun's wake along the main road. 'Downtown' Keel had changed little since my summer in the village, but a few tiny shops had opened and appeared to be making a precarious living. Within a few minutes our procession had turned up the narrow country lane on which my old cottage—the leprechaun's home—was located.

Suddenly, each elemental in our parade swung into formation beside a human. I recognized Dr. Carl's ascetic elf, Peggy's smiling brownie, and Marion's teenage trolls sidle up to them as if to say 'my human'. Their reason for doing this was immediately obvious as we rounded the bend. To my surprise, local elementals of all sizes and varieties lined the lane, cheering, waving banners, and pointing at us. Evidently, we humans were something like stars, as so many of us loved the little people and worked with them. Our elemental partners were enjoying themselves immensely and preened as 'their humans' were shown off. A few goblins, including Molly's, had partnered with humans and occasionally would give them a shove, or blow off their hats, to the cheers of their goblin chums. Meanwhile, my leprechaun crony led the parade and was tipping his hat, nodding and soaking up the accolades—which he obviously felt he deserved—as he'd brought so many elemental-friendly humans home to the village.

Finally, we reached Crumpaun Cottage. *Crumpaun* in Irish means a little mound or hill; it is a fitting name for the cottage that stands on the summit of a hill with a stupendous view overlooking the village and ocean. Unfortunately, an ugly house being built beside the cottage marred the view. The 'posh monstrosity', as the leprechaun called it, was gigantic and looked totally out of place on the lane. You know— complete with pillars and missing only the statues of the Greek gods. This house definitely did not fit anywhere in Ireland, let alone in Keel. The construction site was deserted, and it looked as if it had been for some time. It was easy to see the leprechaun's hand in this, and I thought it unlikely that the building would ever be inhabited.

Crumpaun sat well back from the lane, and was separated from the mausoleum by a large hedge and fence. Local quartz-crystal rocks sat on top of the heavy stone wall protecting the cottage from the lane. That was familiar at least. Surveying the cottage, I discovered that it had undergone a total renovation since I'd lived there. The thick walls had been pointed, meaning that the former plaster had been removed and the stone exposed and re-grouted. Thatch had replaced the slate roof, making it the only thatched cottage in all of Keel. There is a corner stone in the cottage dating from 1742, and the original roof might well have been thatch, even though the most common roofs at the time were made of sod.

Crumpaun Cottage and me

"I see that you like me improvements," commented my pal, puffing himself up and pointing towards his cottage.

"Yes, it's terrific," I assured him, meaning every word.

The cottage reverberated with energy, testifying to how well the changes suited it. A woman, who used to summer in Achill as a child and whose uncle was a local doctor, currently owns it. She and her husband live in Dublin, and they come to the cottage only in the summers and on long weekends. All in all, Lloyd had the perfect setup, which, I had no doubt, he'd had a part in arranging.

Continuing our stroll along the lane, the leprechaun wagged his finger in the direction of the new bungalows being built and, shaking his head in annoyance, remarked, "'Progress' is coming to Keel. Since the country has joined the European Common Market, the standard of livin' has 'risen' in Ireland."

My heart went out to him, but who could blame the locals for seeking the prosperity that had eluded them for so many centuries? Progress is a mixed blessing, and the villagers might not know the full cost to them until their peaceful community was gone. I sent a silent prayer that Keel, while embracing prosperity, would be able to keep the hedgerows, lanes, and undeveloped land for the elementals who, in turn, would keep their Craic in the village.

A new building had been erected at the end of the lane to house the local government, and I halted there to give us a much needed toilet break. By now, the majority of our elemental companions had dispersed, although a few still popped in and out of our three-dimensional reality to see if the 'humans' were doing anything of interest. Discovering that we were making very slow progress by their standards, they quickly vanished.

Standing by the side of the lane waiting for the others, I saw Barbara, one of our folks, suddenly trip and fall for no apparent reason. Nearby, a smirking young goblin jumped up and down with glee that he had mastered the art of toppling a human. Getting up, Barbara remarked, "I don't know what happened. All of a sudden my feet went out from under me. It must have been the elementals." How right she was! Fortunately, she was unhurt and the goblin, probably off to brag of his accomplishment to his pals, was no longer in evidence.

"Did you see that?" I asked the leprechaun, after Barbara set off down the road.

"I was hopin' to avoid a mishap, but some of you humans are so ungrounded it makes it easy for the goblins to topple you," he responded defensively. "If she'd get out of her head and into her feet, it wouldn't have happened."

"Is that the only reason elementals would hurt a human?" I retorted, protective of Barbara, and nervous of what could happen to the others.

"I'd not be sayin' that exactly," asserted Lloyd, adopting his scholarly tone. "If humans think a lot of themselves, elementals enjoy givin' 'em a topple, to bring 'em down a peg. Also, if humans ignore us when we're tryin' to get their attention, we'll give 'em a wake-up call. That's what we did for Peggy on The Reek. We gave her a knock on the head to bring her to her senses. She was goin' round and round in her mind in closed circles, so we opened the circle. What humans think of as 'harmin' is, in most cases, helpin' them to rebalance themselves when they're out of whack. Anyway, Barbara's just fine, isn't she?"

Reflecting on his explanation, I waited for the slower walkers. Many of the faster folks had gone ahead to the cemetery located beside the deserted village of Slievemore. The last of us now in tow, we tramped along enjoying the gorgeous, sunny, spring day. Wild irises grew near the little water channels lining the road, and emerald green fields glowed healthily. All nature vibrated with energy.

As Michael had taken a day off with Paddy, I asked Mary's husband, Sean, a local history buff, for information to guide the tour, especially about Slievemore. "Keel and Achill Island have an ancient history," Sean had said, "and research is beginning to indicate that the site of Slievemore has been occupied since approximately 3000 BCE. In the 1940's the archaeologist Mr. Ruaidhri de Valera discovered the remains of a *crannog*, like the late Bronze and Iron Age villages such as Craggaunowen, about four miles from Slievemore and near the Crossroads Inn."

Approaching Slievemore, we saw the remnants of several megalithic tombs dotting the hillside. A pair of majestic quartz-crystal stones marked the entrance to the deserted village. Walking between these guardian stones, we entered the 'lazy beds' where residents, in times past, grew potatoes in raised mounds to keep them from rotting in the boggy soil. These beds are amongst the first in Ireland, and the ruined stone homes, called 'booley houses', were summer residences for locals grazing their cattle. Locals used to keep both sheep and breeds

Rinder

of small cattle that were adapted to the less rich grazing. The 'booley houses' have been deserted since the mid-eighteenth century and a sad veil hangs over Slievemore now.

"In recent years," Sean had told me, "the farmers in Keel have sold off the local cattle in order to buy larger breeds, like the Charolais, which the farmers thought would give more profit per pound. Unfortunately, these larger cattle needed richer grazing than Achill offered and would not calve without extra feed. The farmers realized their error too late and replaced the cattle with sheep. This solution has its own problems, as sheep like to graze only green grass and not the coarser grass in which Achill abounds. At present, this coarser grass is taking over the hills. There are not enough left of the former breeds to rebuild the herds, adding salt to the farmers' wounds."

Zeitdauer
gran

As I was walking, I remembered my conversation with Sean and, picking up my thoughts, the leprechaun said, "It takes thousands of years for plants and animals to adjust to livin' in one place and then you humans, always thinkin' of gettin' more money, upset the balance and destroy all that we have built up. We used to live in Slievemore with the humans and now we never go there."

"Did elementals have anything to do with closing the crystal quarry just above Slievemore?" I inquired, feeling increasingly sad at Lloyd's words.

Zeche, Erzgang

"The humans raped the earth of all the crystal and there's nothing much left for 'em to take now," he responded downcast. "In my ancestor's time, the humans in Slievemore knew how much crystal and peat to take from the hills without hurtin' the land. There was a nice balance with humans respectin' elementals, and leavin' out milk, bread, and honey for us. Things pretty much died when this ended and then the potato famine came."

Torf

The landscape around Slievemore is rich in peat that develops in the boggy, heather-covered ground. Locals from Keel and the neighbouring town of Dooagh still cut this peat for their turf fires, which has a beautiful sweet aroma much favoured by the leprechaun. No central heating for him. A cemetery rests at the foot of the peat hills of Slievemore, and the group waited for me there.

"I'll see you at the dolmen. I'll not be goin' to the graveyard as it's a bit crowded with all of 'em unhappy dead folk millin' about," my elemental pal said, with an immense shiver, and disappeared.

Our walkers entered the oldest section of the graveyard where, amidst the weeds, wildflowers, and overgrown grasses, an old cross and grave markers have sunk into the boggy earth. Here, the ghosts of local people who starved during the potato famine still hovered, speaking of their painful deaths to all who would listen. In this unkempt part of the graveyard we spread out to pray for peace for the restless dead and to help them to move on.

"Yer folks are doin' good work," I heard my absent leprechaun friend comment. "They are removin' the old hurts to the Earth, and other beins', and we elementals appreciate it and have somethin' special planned to help."

The dark energies surrounding the cemetery lifted with his kind words and the sun shone brightly again. Ute, Wolfgang, and other tired folks, unused to so much walking, returned to the Unicorn where Mary and Sean would have a cup of tea and homemade scones waiting. The rest of us continued along the country road until we reached a steep path on the left, which would take us to the dolmen.

As promised, the leprechaun and the other elementals were lining the ascent. In his hand my pal held the bottle of *Emergency Energy* and, when people flagged, Lloyd and his friends threw some drops on them, much as priests would dole out Holy Water. With their support, our sore-legged pilgrims, exhausted from their walk up Croagh Patrick the previous day, climbed to the megalithic tomb.

The wind was gusting fiercely at the top of the exposed hillside and, trying to keep warm, we wrapped ourselves in our jackets and pulled on hats. The wind, much more powerful than the breeze on the road, let us know that elemental forces were involved. In contrast, the elemental's hair and clothes remained unruffled. With the cool detachment of doctors preparing to undertake brain surgery, the serious older elf accompanying Dr. Carl, Kirsten's beautiful female elf, Peggy's little sweetie, and a few gnomes and leprechauns spread out in a protective circle around the humans. Luckily, the young trolls had left the goblin gang and accompanied their elemental elders. None of the elementals spoke aloud to each other, but communicated telepathically what to do.

Poised, waiting for the exact right moment, the leprechaun pointed his walking stick at the sky and called down the wind even more fiercely on our humans. As he did so, the vortex of energy and wind increased, sucking dark etheric and astral debris from our auras and swirling it away. Our auras were left cleansed and sparkling.

Finished with his ritual, he nodded at me to explain about the dolmen. Raising my voice to be heard over the gusting wind, I said, "Dolmens, for those of you who don't know, are megalithic tombs built and used from 4000 to 2000 BCE. This dolmen is called a court cairn, so named for a U-shaped open court. The wider end is lined with slabs or dry-stone walls. Archaeologists debate the meaning and function of these tombs. They are believed to be burial sites for important people, and where religious services, including sacrifices, were conducted."

Giant's Grave Dolmen

Relating my personal experiences, I continued, "The summer I lived in the cottage I spent a wet night in this very dolmen, experiencing an initiation of sorts. Many dolmens have guardians, who were, while alive, the most powerful people in their tribes, and whose purpose is to protect the people of the area, both presently and in the past. Many of these guardians are etherically still in these dolmens. If you go inside, you might be able to access your own past lives from this megalithic period, and learn about the life of the people of that time. This is what happened to me."

"Could we enter now?" asked Kirsten, our beautiful, tall woman who loved new experiences, just like the elves she resembled. Unknown to her, the two teenage trolls had already pushed past her and were busy trying to beat each other through the entrance. Being so broad, they were now stuck. Trolls love stone, it's their element after all, and so the dolmens were of special interest to them. Finally, the troll who appeared slightly larger (this is like comparing Mt. Everest to K2) pushed his way inside, followed immediately by the smaller one.

"Yes, if you feel drawn to do so," I replied to Kirsten, hoping that the trolls had left some room inside. "Just remember that, aware of it or not, the energies will affect you. So make certain that the guardians give you permission before entering."

Kirsten bent down and entered the dolmen, while Diana and others came forward and silently waited their turn. Some folks had no desire to do so and sat quietly in contemplation. The dolmen, given the name the Giant's Grave, was little known and seldom visited, so we had privacy and time to experience the energies. Gradually, one by one, individuals left to walk back to the Unicorn. Elves, gnomes, and brownies accompanied 'their' humans, and I was reassured to see that goblins were not among them. The young trolls had not come out of the Giant's Grave and, looking inside for them, I remembered that dolmens are often portals to other places and times. The teenagers had obviously gone on their own trip.

Alone, I lay down on the hillside letting the earth of Achill re-energize me. I treasured those moments by myself because when I'm leading a mystical tour, much as I love it, I'm with folks from breakfast until bedtime. That said, one of the disappointments on the present tour was that I had little time to visit with my fellow travellers to chat about their experiences and what they were enjoying. Yes, there were snippets during meals, and from these I knew that many folks loved Achill and Croagh Patrick and were having good experiences. However, too often my time was devoted to sorting out unanticipated problems, and I found this frustrating and missed the social time.

With that thought in mind, I descended the hill and slowly wandered back towards Keel. Instead of taking the low road into the village, I turned up the lane past Crumpaun Cottage to see if my former neighbours, Maureen and Brendan, were around. I wanted to speak to them of their Mum, my dear friend Mrs. O'Toole, who had looked after me the summer that I'd lived at Crumpaun. Every evening on her way home from the cows—or 'coos' as she referred to them—Mrs. O'Toole, with her feet in wellies and wearing an old dress held together with a safety pin, would come and light my turf fire. Unable to learn the gift of lighting the peat by myself, I'd have frozen if not for her kind heart. Mrs. O'Toole had died a few years ago and, for me, her passing marked the close of an era and the old Irish ways. As I walked along the lane, each step I took reminded me of her.

Passing by Crumpaun Cottage, the leprechaun emerged beside me. Removing his hat and bowing like a chivalrous gentleman, he swung me through the gate and into the yard. The owners were not home, but I was concerned that the neighbours would see me trespassing.

"Always mindin' what others think," my friend teased, seating himself on the grass and patting the ground for me to do the same. No sooner had I sat down than he vanished with a mysterious smile on his face. I was on the point of rising when his mate, the female leprechaun who lived with him in the cottage, came out the door and walked toward me. She looked very different from the last time I had seen her. Her former long dress and old clogs had been replaced by a skirt, which fell just below her knees, and shoes that would have found company in human stores of the 1940's. In fact, her attire looked entirely from that period.

Seeing me notice her new wardrobe, she smiled and said, "Welcome back. You can see that I'm 'eeeemancipated' now."

"What do you mean by 'emancipated'?" I asked, intrigued by her choice of words.

"I have a say with Himself now, 'cos human women are having a say, so why not us?" she continued, crossing her arms across her chest, emphasizing that she was determined in her ways.

Amused, I remembered back to the time when my leprechaun crony had said she was 'silly' and not interested in the serious talks that he and I were having. I wondered how he was making out with his 'emancipated' mate.

"You've made quite a change in our lives," she said, picking up my thoughts. "I'm still milkin' the coos, gatherin' honey, and makin' soda bread like I always did, and he's still lookin' after the poteen (home-made Irish liquor) and the Guinness. So, Himself's got nothin' to complain of."

"What changes have you seen?" I asked, finding her more forthcoming than during our previous encounters.

"We females don't need to card sheep's wool anymore, although most of us still sew for our own pleasure and I made me own dress. I'm considered quite modern in me dress as compared with other females me age," she said proudly. "There's fewer coos and bees so it's harder to get milk and honey now, but at the same time, it's easier 'cos, if we run short, we can hop into the human neighbours for a bite. Still, we like to maintain good relations, so that's a last resort like," she continued with a mischievous twinkle in her eye.

"How are the boys?" I asked. Her two children had been quite young when I'd lived in the cottage and I was eager to hear about them.

"Aren't they a handful, especially the elder?" she answered, rolling her eyes. "He's eatin' mushrooms all the time and dyein' his hair all sorts of colours and hangin' around with some of the goblin thugs. They're teachin' him some bad ways. Himself and I don't know what to do with him!"

Just then the very culprit being discussed popped up beside his mother. He looked about fourteen years of age in human terms, but was probably double that in elemental age. He wore baggy pants down to his knees with multi-coloured socks, and his hair stood on end and flashed green, pink, then yellow, like Christmas tree lights. I guess this was the latest in leprechaun teenage style.

"Mum worries too much," he moaned, tickling his mother in the ribs as he spoke. "I've just been hangin' round me mates in the lane and we're not doin' nothin' wrong. Just a little fun."

"Seems like the same kind of teenage talk that I'd heard coming from human boys his age," I thought to myself, while at the same time wondering if the teenage goblin, who had toppled Barbara, was one of his mates.

"What kind of fun, may I ask?" his mother interjected, looking to me for support. "He's devilin' the coos and sheep."

"We're just paintin' different colours on 'em so the farmers get 'em mixed up. Nothin' so bad, in't it?" replied the teenager, also looking to me for support.

"Great," I thought to myself. "Caught in the middle of a leprechaun family row."

Before I could respond she was on to her next point. "And what about that business at the local?"

"Ye' said ye' weren't goin' to mention that agin," he screamed back at her.

"Well, just for the lady," the female leprechaun said, her colour starting to change into an embarrassed pink. "She's wantin' to know all about us, after all."

The teenager threw me a resentful glare, while Mum continued. "He's been drinkin' a lot from the locals' glasses." With her words she threw me an image of gigantic glasses of Guinness being downed by her son. I wasn't sure how this differed from her eating the good out of the food of her human neighbours, but I wasn't about to say anything.

"As if I'm the first. I bet Da—Lloyd the Grand—did it in his day," he said, emphasizing his father's title with a wee bit of sarcasm.

"Himself wasna a drunk. We've a reputation to keep up with all the guests comin' to see yer father now," she answered, projecting an image of thousands of elves, trolls, and gnomes lined up at her door.

"What do you want to do when you grow up?" I asked the teenager, trying to change the topic and get them back into harmony.

"Either a musician or artist. I haven't decided," he responded, willing to go along with me, although slightly grudgingly.

"So, you won't be following your dad in his work with humans?"

"Not the way he does. He's sooooooo old-fashioned. I wouldn't mind blendin' some human and elemental music. Even though yer stuff is primitive compared to ours, you're quite good at havin' a beat," the young one replied, sending me images of him playing loudly on a drum kit like other teenagers. With those final words he disappeared in a puff of smoke reminiscent of the witch's departure in the film the *Wizard of Oz.*

"What about the younger one?" I asked, turning to his mum and hoping it was good news.

"He's at the telly all the time."

I saw an image of the younger leprechaun sitting in front of what appeared to be an elemental version of a television. He was watching pictures of various kinds of elementals leaping in and out of the screen interacting with him. He seemed as mesmerized as a human child would be at the equivalent age.

"Young ones," I smiled sympathetically.

"Yes, young 'uns," she acknowledged and, nodding to me, vanished.

I was glad to have met my friend's family again, and was thinking how similar the problems were in our two worlds when Lloyd reappeared.

"It's time for that Guinness you promised," said my pal, exerting his full charm.

With those words he dragged me onto the lane where local gnomes, leprechauns, and a few goblins slapped him on the back and congratulated him for a job well done. Many elementals smiled indulgently at me and, surprisingly, even the goblins included me in their celebration, although with more reserve. After all, I was still the 'human.'

"I think we've both earned that pint, don't you?" I said, laughing with the leprechaun as we descended the lane to the pub.

Swinging open the heavy old door, I entered a large, dreary room. Glancing about, I saw that it was abandoned except for Karen and Sheridan, two of our walkers. A dour, middle-aged man was cleaning out the grate prior to lighting a peat fire for the evening.

"It's good to be back in Keel," I said, walking over to him and trying to strike up a conversation.

"Oh," said he, squinting at me out of the corner of his eye.

"Yes, I lived in Crumpaun Cottage one summer," I continued, still hopeful of a chat.

"Oh," said he, raising his eyes to appraise me fully. The landlord made no other reply and returned to the peat.

Seeing the conversation had no chance of igniting, I asked for a drink that many Irish women like. "Could I have a pint of Guinness with black currant and..."

Looking around, I was amazed that my friend had disappeared without his desired Guinness. Then, I realized the reason. I've learned through past experience that most elementals want to be where there's joy and play. The local was too quiet at that early hour to attract him. I was fairly certain that he'd be back on his own later that evening when the pub was hopping. I, however, was happy to have a pint quietly with Karen and Sheridan and, picking up the brimming glass of black brew with a hint of black current purple resting on top, I made my way to their table.

I sipped the froth delighted with the Guinness, my first since coming to Ireland. Guinness is chock full of vitamin B. In fact, it was given to nursing mothers in the old days to build them up after giving birth, so I could easily justify it as a health drink. A strange thing about Guinness is its short shelf life, so buying it outside of Ireland, where it is made, is a dicey proposition. It, like the magic of the Craic and elementals, just doesn't travel well.

Afterwards, as I strolled back to the Unicorn, thoughts of how fond my leprechaun pal was of Mary and her mother came unbidden into my mind. Their families shared a long relationship, which I'd discovered only some eight years earlier, when I'd brought another group to the inn. Mary's Mum, whom Mary and Sean affectionately referred to as the General Manager, was bedridden by that time, and she'd asked to see me.

Entering her room, I was happy to find that she was as sharp as ever. She had a cosy dignity that was warm and efficient, and that kept her customers coming back to the Unicorn year after year. She had on a freshly laundered flowered blouse and looked healthy despite her lack of mobility. As I reached her bed she took my hand in hers and squeezed it. Like Mary, her mum also seemed like family and reminded me of my own beloved grandma. Something in the Irish blood, or karma, opens my heart whenever I think of those women.

"You know," she said, smiling and holding my hand, "when you used to talk about living with a leprechaun in Crumpaun Cottage, I never said anything, but I'd like to tell you something now. My family used to own that cottage and we always called it the faery cottage, so I know what you are talking about when you mention living there with the little people."

That was all she said and all she was going to say. I was struck by her good humour, and by how close-mouthed the Irish are, especially those from the west of Ireland. They'll wait for years to tell you something. Come to think of it, from what I'd seen, even Irish elementals hold their secrets close.

My reverie was cut short. Opening the front door of the Unicorn,

I ran into a deeply concerned Diana who informed me that the local doctor had come to see two of our darlings. "Molly fell in the lane on the way to the cottage and may have broken her arm, and Caitlin's face has swollen up with a terrible burn and blisters."

"Bloody hell," I thought to myself. "First Barbara falling, and now Molly—and the Guinness I drank is starting to kick in."

Making my way to Molly's room, I found her lying on the bed, holding her arm. She was calm—a quality I associated with her— perhaps gained through years of meditation and yoga. Still, her dark eyes revealed her discomfort and confusion.

"What happened?" I asked, sinking down beside her bed to give healing energy to her wounded wing.

"The strangest thing," she replied, holding my hand. "I was walking down the lane when, all of sudden, my feet went out from under me. I was spun in the air, did a hundred and eighty degree turn, and ended up on the ground, facing in the opposite direction."

As a yoga practitioner, Molly was fit and flexible, not a person unsteady on her pinions. The description of her fall sounded like more goblin work to me. I saw by her look and words that she agreed. Likely, the happy goblin, who had accompanied Molly on the pilgrimage up Croagh Patrick and the parade earlier that day, could take the credit.

"What do you make of it?" I asked, knowing that she liked to figure out reasons for occurrences by herself.

"I'm not sure," Molly answered. "But it will come to me. The doctor doesn't think my arm is broken, so I should be all right."

That was good news at least. I only hoped that Molly would find clarity and trust in elementals despite their sometimes roundabout healing practices. Goblins are the bad boys of the elemental kingdom, but no worse than the unloved rascals who populate our own jails. Goblins thrive on rigid thoughts, fears, and negativity, much in the same way as thugs do. However, if you stand up to them and earn their respect through fairness, strict boundaries, and love, they will often respond in kind.

Leaving Molly, I changed quickly for dinner and waited in the dining room for Caitlin to arrive. The poor dear entered late. Her face was a fiery red mess, her mouth blistered and swollen to twice its usual size. Shuffling slowly to a small table, she gently eased herself into the seat. I went to her carrying antihistamines and burn salves in case she wanted them.

Caitlin had trouble talking through her painful lips, "Thank you for the medicines," she mumbled. "It's strange, but I think the wind burned me as much as the sun."

Hearing her words, I was reminded of the ritual that the leprechaun had conducted at the dolmen when the wind had sucked our auras clean.

"We had to work hard on her with our healing techniques, as her head was so damaged from the accident she had some years back. Now you know why we needed all the medical supplies," Lloyd said, dangling the splints and bandages before my eyes.

As he spoke, I remembered that Caitlin had had a very bad car accident a few years earlier that had left her partially brain damaged. She was not fully recovered even now.

"Also, because Caitlin is one of us," continued my friend, "it's harder for her to endure the wind and sun the way you full humans do."

He was referring to the fact that Caitlin is part elemental. There are many hybrid humans who are originally from elemental, angelic, dolphin, and other evolutions. Elementals entered human evolution in order to develop free will and to learn to love. Caitlin, as the leprechaun said, was one of these hybrids.

None of this information would surprise Caitlin, who knew the truth of her elemental connection and whose life in rural upstate New York was devoted to helping the little people. She wore a short, pixyish hairstyle, highlighted with blue streaks, and had magnetic elemental eyes that were a bit slanted and wild. Like many elemental hybrids, she was talented in the arts and was a painter, photographer, and maker of faery homes. Not all elemental hybrids know of their elemental origins, as Caitlin did. Yet many hybrids sense that they are different from other humans.

"Yer right about that," interjected my elemental chum, reading my thoughts. "Yer Man, James the Lep, as you call him, hasn't a clue that he's originally elemental, so he can't control the magic."

"You mean that he didn't intentionally take us into the Craic with his lack of planning for the tour?" I asked.

"To be sure, you humans would say that he's a chaos maker, but it happens around him, rather than through him, 'cos he doesn't understand the laws of the Craic as we full elementals do," replied my friend, puffing himself up with pride.

"Which are ... ?" said I, gesturing for him to continue.

"Not so fast, me girl. You can't learn about the Craic by talkin' about it, but only by livin' it and by lettin' it teach you, which is what we're about with yer folks. Anyway, we're lookin' after yer humans, so don't you worry. You'll have enuf to worry about tomorrow."

As he left, his words echoed in my mind, leaving a poignant silence.

Having been raised on the axiom 'an ounce of prevention is worth a pound of cure,' I decided to head off future problems. Ever an optimist I, like the poet Dylan Thomas, was not prepared to go 'quietly into that good night' without trying, once again, to get our tour back on the track that our group and myself would prefer. You know, the one where we would see great sacred sights and have a fun holiday full of meaningful rituals—and all with ease. So, as dinner was winding down, I made my way to Michael, Paddy, and Brian's table.

From my former tours, I was used to our guides' eating and social-izing with the group, but none of the Big Three wanted to do this.

I recognized more and more that they had no real understanding, or sympathy, for the spiritual nature of our tour and that, for them, believing in elementals was definitely out of the question. Michael, Paddy, and Brian had likely thought that they would have an easy trip with my giving them the itinerary and their knowing Ireland so well. It was unlikely that they had ever stopped to consider the reason people take the tour and perhaps, just perhaps, why the leprechaun was having fun with their preconceived business plan.

It saddened me that both they and our pilgrims were missing opportunities to share their lives. Still, there is no point wishing for what isn't going to change. Therefore, I decided to focus on making sure that the group received what was promised in the written itinerary and which, hopefully, the four of us would be able to agree on. I pulled out the paper to review the next day's sites with them.

"I don't know where Carrowmore is," said our driver Paddy, looking at the itinerary as if for the first time.

"Michael, do you know?" I asked our guide hopefully.

"Well I've been there, but I couldn't say where it is exactly," Michael replied noncommittally.

"Brian, what about you?" I asked, in danger of losing my patience.

"I'll go ahead tomorrow morning, find it, and call Paddy on his cell to give him directions," was Brian's response.

"What about Carrowkeel?" I asked, thinking ahead to the second site.

"It's too far. We won't be able to go there and still get to our hotel in Northern Ireland by the evening," retorted Paddy, pointing to where we were staying the next night. A location, by the way, which James the Lep and Brian of Gallows had changed from my original plan.

"What about the Holy Well of Tobernalt near Lough Gill?" I asked, indicating the third item on our itinerary.

"Never been there."

"Never been there."

"Never been there," were the three answers around the table.

Paddy finished off the conversation nicely. "If it's up in this area"—he thrust his index finger at the map—"the bus is too big for the roads, so we can't go."

All three of them, united in their decision, nodded sagely, reinforcing their point that we were going only to Carrowmore, one of the three promised sites. They did not budge from their seats, leaving me with the unpleasant duty of informing the others. Unhappy faces resulted and tempers flared. People felt, yet again, that they were not receiving what had been promised.

Max, the gallant group member who had helped Marion down the mountain, having participated in my well-organized previous tours, was shocked by what was happening. He does not suffer fools gladly and is quick to react. His face became redder and his jaw set. As soon as I had finished speaking, he leapt out of his seat beside his wife, Melanie, stormed into the other room and started giving Brian a piece of his mind. I confess that a part of me would have been pleased if Max, or the leprechaun, or even a helpful goblin, had clomped Brian on the head to knock some sense into him. However, another part of me—albeit a continually shrinking part—was relieved that this didn't happen.

Meanwhile, unhappy pilgrims with down-turned mouths muttered together in small groups as they rose to leave. Others stoically tried to make the best of a bad lot and departed quietly, and some, like Melanie and Peggy, gave me glances of sympathy as they passed. Above the sounds of the tables being cleared angry words emerged from the other room. "Unacceptable…," "not what we paid for…," "get your act together…," and "totally unprofessional," accused Max.

Knowing that there was no point arguing with Max in his present state of mind, the three kept their heads down and eyes averted. Max's thunder soon abated and discussion ensued, although nothing had changed in the end. By now it was 10:30 and I, tired from a long and full day, did not look forward to a difficult morrow. Walking back to my room, I reflected on my learning for Friday the thirteenth, which our fellows and fellas had survived. What struck me the most was that, even in the midst of the happiness we were experiencing on Achill, we still had painful lessons to learn. Molly and Caitlin suffered physical pain, while Max and many fellow pilgrims, including myself, experienced psychological distress when our expectations were not met.

Just like the best swords, which are fired and struck by the blacksmith again and again, we were being honed and strengthened as our attachments to comforts and things going smoothly were being removed one by one. Call me a Pollyanna, if you like, but I felt the touch of grace in every turn of the Craic, wielded lovingly and uncompromisingly by Lloyd and his mates.

As I undressed and slipped into bed, my last thought was of how lucky we were to have warm beds, full stomachs, and good friends on our pilgrimage. How few pilgrims had it so good?

chapter six

Carrowmore and Faery Stories

R ising early, I walked quietly down the hall and out the side door to the beach. Peggy, Dr. Carl, and Kirsten were doing the same and, by unspoken agreement, we continued by ourselves. Listening to the roaring waves, I meandered nostalgically along the sand to the cliff at the end of the bay.

"You should come back to Keel more often if you love it so much," said the leprechaun, appearing by my side.

"Yes, it's true," I acknowledged. "I'm going to do that in the future."

"Silly," chortled my friend, sending me an image of exhausting plane flights. "You can travel just by thought as elementals do. You've been around us long enuf to know that by now."

"I know I can," I replied. "Even science has proven that we create our reality by our thoughts. However, it's a big step for humans to leap from believing this in theory to being able to manifest that reality all the time as you elementals do. I, like most humans, love to do things physically. You've heard our expression, 'Seeing is believing.'"

"That's why we're teachin' yer humans how to create whatever reality they want."

"Which means...?" I interjected, asking for clarification.

"Humans get these fixed ideas that everythin' should happen accordin' to yer expectations. How borin' is that? What do you learn if you know exactly what's goin' to happen? Nothin'!" asserted the leprechaun. "We elementals are helpin' you by breakin' all yer expectations, just like our goblin friend did with that Molly girl yesterday, so that you can learn to accept everythin' that happens as the perfect thing. Then you'll have an open mind with no attachment to gettin' yer way, so you'll be in harmony with natural and divine laws."

Listening to his words, I remained silent while he continued. "Some humans in the group are doing very well with these lessons; others are resistin' them and are therefore unhappy and angry. If they'd leave off resistin', their pilgrimage would go much easier."

"Is there anything I can do to help either them, or myself, with accepting 'what is' without resistance?" I inquired, preferring, like most humans, to learn the lesson fast and painlessly.

"Today, on the bus, explain to 'em what's happenin'; that's all you need to do. They wanted to get to know us, so we are givin' 'em exactly what they asked for," the mischievous elemental guffawed.

"And you could tell 'em what great manifesters they are, that they manifested the pilgrimage, just as they needed it," he continued, gasping for breath, holding his ample stomach, all in all thoroughly enjoying the situation.

Irish are known for their black humour and for laughing when things go wrong; they have most likely picked this up from leprechauns. As I come from an Irish family, I appreciate black humour, and my friend soon had me laughing along with him. Just as quickly as he had arrived, he disappeared, leaving me to wander back to the Unicorn in a jolly mood.

After another terrific breakfast with 'real' porridge—lucky for Lloyd and us—we went outside to sing and dance. Katje, Dr. Carl's gracious wife, led the dance. Imagine what Princess Grace would have looked like in her mid-sixties, if she had married an eccentric German doctor and raised six children without the benefit of nannies, and you will have a feeling for what Katje is like. Born in the States, she spent much of her childhood living abroad until Dr. Carl, seeing a loving, spiritual soul with the beauty of a model, claimed her.

Katje gracefully led us in a dance to honour the four elements of the Earth. Nature spirits love singing and dancing, and this was the best gift we could give them to show our appreciation for their welcome on Achill.

Kirsten and Dr. Carl's elves lent grace to their human partners, while Marion's trolls tripped over their immense feet trying to keep in time with the music. Peggy's brownie turned out to be a skilled dancer and was beaming brightly as she led Peggy through unknown steps. Ute and Wolfgang, familiar with the dance that Katje was leading, were joined by gnomes and flower faeries playfully weaving in and out between them. Molly, still recuperating from her fall the previous day, sat on a bench cradling her arm.

Meanwhile, the young goblin, who had tripped Barbara the day before, stood restlessly beside Molly's goblin who bore a striking resemblance to him—like father, like son. Happily, the goblins had finished their shenanigans and were on best behaviour. Seamus, the young leprechaun I'd met the previous day, joined the human circle and, keeping their time, was emulating them perfectly.

Having thanked the elementals, we humans headed for the bus. "Seamus, are you coming with us?" I asked, as he sauntered along beside me.

"No. I'm looking after things here while Lloyd leads your group," Seamus chuckled. Just then, Lloyd strolled by us and onto the bus, carrying a gigantic, emerald-green suitcase with the words *Human Pilgrimage of Ireland* blazoned on the side.

"Seamus, what is your relationship with Lloyd?" I asked with more than a little curiosity.

"I'm his apprentice and he's teaching me to work cooperatively with humans. He's the expert on humans among leprechauns. My father knows Himself and was able to get me the job."

"I can't help but notice, Seamus, that you seem better educated than my friend, who is a bit of a diamond in the rough."

"I'm a *modern* leprechaun from the north and I can read books, just as humans do," Seamus replied with the same kind of pride I'd noticed in his mentor, Lloyd. "My Da took me to human places when I was a young 'un, so I'd feel comfortable with humans."

"That's fascinating," I responded, intrigued to hear how leprechauns were adjusting to the modern world.

Reading my thoughts, Seamus quickly steered me into the direction that he wanted me to take. "Actually, I'm a bit too human, if you know what I mean, so I've been sent by my Da to Achill to learn more about my own culture."

I couldn't pursue this conversation as the bus was ready to leave. Mary and Sean had come to send us off, so I said a quick goodbye to Seamus. Mary gave me a big hug, and seeing me a bit weepy, said, "You're always welcome and we've loved having your group. They are lovely, but why don't you come by yourself for a holiday next year."

They had overheard the problems with the Big Three the previous night—How could they not?—and tactfully were acknowledging my difficulties, without actually saying it. How very Irish!

"I will come next year," I replied to her suggestion, "and then we can have more of a visit."

"Come early in the season so we'll not be so busy," Mary requested. "Mum always spoke about you and your livin' in our old cottage with the little people. It was so good that you saw her that year before she passed."

With her last words she gave me another hug and I hopped on the bus, too choked up to reply. Leaving Mary and Keel was difficult; I was safe and supported there, and now I felt that I was heading even more into the unknown.

The ride to Carrowmore was a blur as I still grieved leaving Achill, such a pull it has on me. We arrived in Carrowmore to discover that Brian had arranged an expert guide to take us through the site. Even so, it was not smooth sailing. Brian didn't know that we had paid his partner, James the Lep, for the entrances to Carrowmore, and he began to ask each person to pay a second time.

"No, don't," I said, nipping that idea in the bud. "I'll pay for everyone again now, but please check with James, as I've already given him the money to cover our group's entrance."

"One down and two to go," murmured the leprechaun, leaving me to wonder what the next two hurdles were.

Now, a wee bit of history about why I'd wanted our folks to see Carrowmore, and thanks be to the goddess that the leprechaun agreed. I was beginning to get the feeling that we'd not be there without his co-operation. Carrowmore is one of the most ancient Stone Age sites in Europe, dating back to 5000 BCE, which is 2000 years earlier than its more famous Irish cousin, Newgrange. Carrowmore is a beautiful site, surrounded on all sides by mountains, upon which are located some forty-five stone circles and passage graves. The largest passage grave is Queen Maeve's Cairn, also known as Knocknarea.

Maeve, also called Madbh, was a pre-Celtic Queen of Ireland. According to Ireland's earliest tales, she had many husbands—all of whom became King of Connaught through marriage to her. Maeve owned land and wealth, which was typical of the independence belonging to women in Ireland in pre-historical times when the goddess was worshipped.

"Maeve's one of our ancestors," Lloyd murmured to me, as we strolled behind the guide. "That's why she's called the Queen of the Faeries."

"Do you mean that she was an elemental?" I asked, now understanding that Carrowmore and Knocknarea were sacred sites for elementals.

"She was one of the Tuatha Dé Danann," he answered. "They are the ancestors of our present day elementals."

"The Celts believed that the Tuatha Dé Danann race went underground into the faery mounds, but that's just a metaphor for them being replaced by the Celts, the conquering race, isn't it?" I inquired, checking to see if I had the correct facts.

"That's the right of it," Lloyd agreed.

Just at that moment, the Carrowmore guide said, "It has recently been discovered that ninety-eight percent of the Irish people native to the west coast can be traced back to the original settlers who came across a land bridge from Siberia over 50,000 years ago."

The guide continued, "This discovery has overturned the previous belief that the Irish in the west of Ireland were Celts who had come in successive waves from Europe. It seems, according to recent evidence, that these waves never reached the west of Ireland genetically, although the local population adopted the language and many customs of the Celts."

"That's interesting," I commented to Lloyd. "I've heard before that an early population both in Ireland and western Britain had a genetic marker different from the Celts. This source said that these people were Indo-Europeans, with dark hair and eyes, and of average height, who emigrated west, not from Siberia, but from the Iberian Peninsula during the Mesolithic and Neolithic periods. I'm inclined to agree with this source, as I think these early people in the west of Ireland and Britain might well have originated in Atlantis.

"Is it possible," I continued, "that the prevalent psychic gifts of 'second sight' and the belief in little people, which are found in the west of Ireland, came through the genetic link to this older race, and not through the Celts?"

"Two down and one to go," said my friend in my ear, as the guide started walking us back to the entrance to re-board the bus.

It would be a long drive to Northern Ireland and, to use our time wisely, I asked our guide, Michael, if he would speak about the little people. To his credit, he was a fount of knowledge, as far as book learning went, and I was grateful that he liked to share his stories with us, which our curious travellers appreciated. The leprechaun— obviously an elemental expert—sat in the seat opposite me, eager to pass judgment on Michael's stories. Turning on the microphone, Michael began.

"There are three stories of the origin of faeries," he said in a scholarly tone reminiscent of the leprechaun's own tone. "According to the ninth century *Book of Armagh*, they are the old gods of the Earth who were widely worshipped in pagan Ireland. A second source says, they're fallen angels who were thrown out of Heaven because they sat on the fence during Lucifer's rebellion. A third theory states that they are survivors of the Tuatha Dé Danann, who brought a high culture to Ireland from ancient Greece, and who were conquered by later races so that they've now gone underground."

My leprechaun colleague held a large scorecard on which was written, at the top of two columns, the words *Human* and *Himself*. As Michael spoke, his words appeared in the column under *Human* with green check marks, and red Xs appeared next to those words that indicated the leprechaun's judgment of Michael's knowledge. The 'fallen angel' story was totally crossed out by red Xs while the Tuatha Dé Danann theory received a combination of red and green marks.

"The Tuatha Dé Danann, our ancestors," Lloyd whispered to me, "can only live in misty places, and there are very few of these places left on the planet. I want to talk about the Tuatha Dé Danann later on."

Glancing at the scorecard, I glimpsed that the leprechaun's words were written in green under the name *Himself*, showing that all his ideas were correct.

Michael continued, "The most important celebrations for the faeries happen on *Beltane*, which is the first day of May; on Midsummer Day, which is June 21ˢᵗ; on *Lughnasa*, which is the harvest festival of August 1ˢᵗ; and on *Samhain*, which Americans call Halloween."

On Lloyd's score sheet I saw a green check mark after Michael's words. My pal nudged me and said quietly, "On the days that Michael mentioned, the gates are open between the worlds. Humans can come to our elemental dimension through those gates, or we can go to the human world. It's easiest to do this in stone circles and the like." More green check marks appeared in the column under *Himself*.

"A faery wind can take up children, and metal objects, and hit you with a 'bolt'," Michael continued, reminding me of the wild wind that we'd experienced the day before at the dolmen. I didn't need to view the scorecard to check on the accuracy of his words.

Michael explained, "Be careful of wandering faery paths, for, if you meet the faeries, they can either give you a boon or do you damage." The 'damage' part of Michael's words had certainly played out the previous day with Caitlin and Molly, and I noticed, in Michael's tone, that he was underrating the possibility of a boon. Glancing at the leprechaun, I saw his face turn a cross red at what he took to be Michael's slight.

While the leprechaun strove to regain his neutrality, Michael mentioned the many kinds of faeries. "There are *banshees* who are faery women associated with royal houses, especially Munster, and who foretell the death of kings and how kings will do in battle."

My friend, with a great show of generosity, gave Michael a green check mark.

"Then there's the *pooka* who appears as a crippled old man where

I come from in the Mourne Mountains. When the farmers gather in the grain, they always leave something in the field, which they call the 'pooka's share.' "

"So they should," interjected Lloyd. "If humans want to have good luck, they had best leave out food for elementals, like porridge and honey, then there's milk and Guinness and ..."

He was interrupted by Michael's next words, "In other parts of Ireland a pooka might be seen as an eagle, a goat, or a horse."

"I'd say pookas are somethin' like a horse, but not exactly a horse," swore the leprechaun with authority, adding green checks both to his and Michael's side of the scorecard.

"Michael, could you tell us about leprechauns?" I asked, hoping to tease my leprechaun pal.

"I'd be happy to," he replied genially. "Leprechauns belong to the group of solitary faeries, as they like to keep to themselves. The name 'leprechaun' might be derived from the Irish *leith bhrogan* for shoemaker, or it may lie in *luacharmán* meaning pygmy because of its small size."

You can guess which definition my friend preferred.

Michael resumed his commentary. "Leprechauns are the bankers of the faeries and know where all the money in Ireland, even from early Viking and Christian times, is hidden. Even the *siddhe* (the royal caste of elementals) come to leprechauns to get money for gifts."

"Very true. Very true," the leprechaun puffed himself up with pride, while adding another green check mark to Michael's side of the ledger.

"Female leprechauns do not appear to exist," Michael said, proceeding into the shaky area of sexuality. "Not having females, male leprechauns are believed to be offspring of humans and faeries."

"Have you ever heard such rubbish?" admonished my friend, striking out Michael's words with a gigantic red X. "Just because we don't talk about our private business, like some folks"—he huffed in indignation, nodding in Michael's direction—"that one thinks there's something queer about us."

My attention was drawn back to Michael, who was proceeding into even more dicey matters. "Because faeries have trouble having children, they often steal human children and leave an ugly, deformed changeling, in place of the human child. When I was a child, my father left his coat across the foot of my bed to keep the faeries from taking me. That's the way we do it in the Mourne Mountains, but open iron tongs, or a crucifix, could also be used for protection."

As Michael spoke of his personal experience, I began to understand his antipathy towards faeries, and why he kept a goodly distance from our group's desire for actual encounters with the little people. Deep down he might think he was a changeling, and given his physical build that was entirely possible. I did not have time to follow this thought, as Lloyd broke in.

"Thank the goddess the giant is finished," he said, getting his own back at Michael's latest slur.

Trying to make peace between them, I leaned over and asked Michael, "How much of what you told us do you believe?"

"Well," he answered. "In Ireland there are two kinds of truth—the relative truth and the absolute truth. Irish stories specialize in the relative truth, for the absolute truth is too hard to take."

Chuckles erupted throughout the bus, as we laughed at Michael's definition of the two kinds of truth.

"At least the giant's got that right," granted the leprechaun, grinning from ear to ear.

"Ah! I get it. The relative truth is the fuzzy truth of the Craic that elementals love to play in. The absolute truth, on the other hand, is the harsh black and white reality that humans prefer," I said to my elemental pal who laughed in agreement at my deduction.

While our mood was buoyant with humour, I decided to speak

about elementals. Borrowing the microphone from Michael, I stood up.

"Folks," I commenced, "a lot of the 'difficulties' that we are experiencing arise from the elementals teaching us about non-attachment." I looked meaningfully at you-know-who as I said this, since he seemed to be having his own problems with his non-attachment to a great deal of what Michael had said.

"We need to learn to live fully in the moment, and with no expectations, in order to open to the Craic, which the elementals are creating for us. Elementals will push every button until we are unattached to having things our own way," I elaborated, while simultaneously sending Lloyd images of Michael and other humans pushing his buttons. Non-attachment, after all, is for all beings to learn.

"Elementals," I explained, "help all beings to grow into what they really are. For example, elementals are able to see the uniqueness of an individual oak tree, even when it's still an acorn, and work with that plan to help the oak to grow. In the same way, elementals see your potential greatness and know how to help you to become who you truly are. Elementals look at the quickest, most efficient way to achieve their goal, even if that is sometimes painful for you."

Molly, Caitlin, and others appeared to be deep in thought as I spoke.

"This tour," I concluded, "is pushing every button in us. These elementals are fond of us, or they would not have committed to accompanying us on our tour. They want to co-create with humans to help heal the Earth. For this to happen, both elementals and humans need to trust each other, even though we do not always understand one another's ways."

"That just about sums it up," Lloyd said, as I sat back down. He approved my message, both for the humans and elementals.

"Do you think my words will help our folks to learn the lesson?"

"It will help some; we'll help the others," replied my elemental friend in a noncommittal manner. "By the way, that's three out of three for today. You got the last point for teachin' me." He smiled before disappearing.

We had crossed the border into Northern Ireland and were just entering Belleek, where we'd stay for the next two nights.

chapter seven

Devenish, Devas, and the holy Spirit on Pentecost

I awoke the next day in high spirits as it was Pentecost, my favourite day of the year. For those of you whose memory needs a bit of assistance, Pentecost commemorates the biblical event when the fire of the Holy Spirit descended on the heads of the disciples of Jesus. The Holy Spirit gave each of the disciples spiritual gifts that would allow them to teach the gospel. I have always felt very close to the Holy Spirit and have had many amazing things happen on Pentecost. I hoped, based on my past experiences, that this day would be a high point in the tour. I had expectations, a dangerous thing to have with the leprechaun in high gear pricking expectation bubbles. Still, I'd like to share one of these Pentecostal experiences, so you can understand why I was optimistic about that day.

Several years ago, on a former tour of Ireland, our group was staying in Bellinter House, a wonderful convent run by the Sisters of Sion in the sacred Boyne Valley, a few minutes from the Hill of Tara. We'd been there for several nights as I had led a weekend workshop devoted to peace and reconciliation. The day before Pentecost, Beth, the Mother Superior, invited me to lead the Pentecostal service for the nuns, locals, and our group.

"It would be very non-traditional," I said, chuckling at her invitation. "Are you sure you want this?"

"Oh, some of our nuns need shaking up," Beth replied. "I think it would be just the thing."

"We could place objects on the altar for the four elements: flowers for earth, a bowl of water, candles for fire, and a feather for air. Then we could gather in a spiral around the altar, not in rows like you're used to. Every person could choose an angel card to discover his or her Pentecostal gift. Each angel card has nice words on it, like *love* or *grace*, so it would be a positive experience. Are you sure this would be all right?" I asked, still dubious.

"It's perfect," she answered, smiling her approval.

The next day I set up the chapel as Beth and I had agreed, and, one by one, the nuns entered. One of the older nuns, Mary by name, didn't like me. Mary knew that I was the leader of what she thought of as 'radicals'. Some of us weren't even Christians, let alone Catholics, after all! To indicate her displeasure Mary, who served the food in the dining room, always glared at me and gave me smaller portions than others received.

As luck would have it, Mary, dressed in her traditional black habit, was one of the first nuns to enter the chapel. She took one look at the spiral of chairs leading to a central altar and huffed her annoyance. I gave her a candle to carry, which she accepted as fittingly Christian, I suppose, but she refused the angel cards, probably relegating them to a pagan category. Mary took a seat as close to the door as possible to do a quick getaway, I presumed, if I did anything unacceptable to her. The rest of the nuns, local people, and members of our tour soon entered and took their seats.

"Could someone please close the chapel doors?" I requested, pointing towards the heavy oak doors.

When one of the gentlemen had done this, I began praying aloud. "I ask that the Holy Spirit be with us."

With these words, the solid oak doors flew open. You could have heard a pin drop in the room. People were astonished because the doors did not open to the outside, but to an inner hall in the convent where there was no wind.

The same gentleman, without being asked, walked over to the doors, re-closed them, and made sure they were tightly secured.

I began again. "May the Holy Spirit bless us today," I prayed fervently aloud.

The heavy doors blew open again and a wind swept by us. People gasped, holding their breath in awe, and Mary started calling out in ecstasy, "The Holy Spirit, the Holy Spirit is with us!"

Waiting for silence to return to the room, the man walked to the doors and closed them a third time. I began once again, and we felt the blessing of the Spirit remain with us through the service. When it was finished Mary, radiating joy, came towards me and took my hands in hers.

"In over eighty years," she said, "that's the only time I've had such an experience of the Spirit. Thank you so much."

I, myself, was overcome as much as anyone and was especially happy that Mary, after years of devoting her life to God, had experienced the Holy Spirit. In a few minutes Mary excused herself to get the dinner ready. Later, when I passed Mary in the food queue, she gave me a big smile and heaped a gigantic amount of food on my plate.

"That was Mary's way of showing appreciation," I thought, amused at the memory.

Reflecting on this and other powerful, positive Pentecostal experiences, I wondered what fabulous events would transpire on the present day. After all, my angel card for the pilgrimage was 'grace', another name for the Holy Spirit. I was not surrendering my expectations of happiness, which was like waving a red flag at a bull, as a willing leprechaun continued teaching me non-attachment.

The first thing that happened was that our visit to White Island to see the pagan fertility statue of *Sheila-na-gig* was cancelled. The site was closed that day, something that James the Lep and Brian—Why would I be surprised?—had just discovered. I was relieved that we would be able to visit the other two promised sites. On any other tour, I would have been horrified to miss even one site. By contrast, on the present pilgrimage I was grateful that we could visit two out of three sites. Isn't it interesting how our standards change to accommodate circumstances? It reminds me of the various stages in the process of dying. I was still in the bargaining stage of this process, one step after anger, not yet into total depression, and dare I say, two steps removed from acceptance.

Our first stop was a boat trip to Devenish Island on Lower Lough Erne to see monastic ruins dating from the sixth century. Our bus arrived in good time to discover that we needed to wait for another group to join us. There were no complaints about waiting, as many of us were happy to use the public toilets, as the toilets on our bus continued to be off limits. Oh, life's simple pleasures! When the other tour arrived, together we boarded the fifty-six-seater boat called *The Kestrel*.

"All's going well," I thought to myself, as the captain, dressed in official hat and jacket, turned on his microphone to commence his commentary.

"Welcome... *buzz*... *hisssss*... ladies and ge... *buzz*... I... *buzz,* captain... *hiss*... "

Everyone waited patiently for the sound to be corrected and, when it wasn't, the passengers cried out for the captain to fix it. With typical Irish humour, I was tickled to note that these inconveniences were not just limited to our group, but encompassed the other tour as well. I caught myself wondering if the other group had leprechauns on their tour, or if our elementals had temporarily taken them under their wing.

"I'll give you two guesses, and the first doesn't count," the leprechaun smirked, standing beside the captain and monkeying with the microphone knobs.

Minutes later, volume surging up and down accompanied by lots of fiddling with knobs and electrical plugs, the captain recommenced his explanation. "Welcome… *buzz*… *hiss*… as I was saying… *buzz*… our trip today… Devenish… monks… round tower… *hiss*…"

On and on the captain rambled, but none of the passengers had the faintest clue what he was talking about. However, we didn't have to worry about his broadcast for long because a few minutes later we came to a lock that controlled traffic flow, and discovered a gigantic tourist cruiser blocking our passage. The tourists aboard were having great difficulty figuring out how the lock worked, until finally our first mate got off our boat to help them out. The clock was already ticking on our leisurely visit to Devenish. Fortunately, it was another beautiful, sunny day and the water was calm, so we didn't need to worry about seasickness.

On our way again, we soon reached Devenish and were preparing to disembark, when the captain, realizing we hadn't understood his talk over the microphone, turned in frustration to face us.

Raising his voice, he roared, "You will only be able to stay on the island for thirty minutes, as I have to get back for the next group." While yet another disappointment was sinking in, the captain added, "Anyone who is not here in thirty minutes will be left behind."

Some of our folks, on the verge of rebelling against yet another injustice, rolled their eyes in displeasure at his words. The captain stepped off the boat, followed by panicky people, racing up the hill, trying to fit in all the sights in the allotted time. The monastic setting was beautiful, not that we had time to enjoy it. The eighty-one-foot

(twenty-five-meter) round tower on Devenish is one of the finest
in Ireland. It was built in the ninth century to store treasures and to
repel attacks from the Vikings. Diana, Kirsten, and our most fit ones
climbed the tower and earned a panoramic view for their efforts.
Hannah, Sara, and less physically gifted folks visited the ruins of St.
Mary's Priory.

Devenish Round Tower

Because of our short amount of time, I decided to skip the Pentecostal ritual that I had planned. Instead, hoping to salvage a little from the given constraints, I offered to lead a Cherokee movement meditation for those individuals who wished it. We gathered near an unusual high cross and had just enough time for the instructions before the boat whistle sounded.

Rushing back to the boat, I was greeted by our tour's elemental co-leader standing on the gangplank, wearing an oversized captain's hat and hurrying people aboard. Clearly, he wasn't interested in our lingering at a monastic site, and I wondered if he was up to something. I didn't have a chance to ask him, as he vanished right after we boarded. We'd find out shortly; there was no point hurrying the inevitable.

Amazingly, the cruise back was uneventful, and I enjoyed watching the water birds on the quiet lough. Too quickly, it seemed, we arrived at the dock where other clients already awaited our boat. Re-boarding our bus, Paddy drove to a lovely park in the small town of Belcoo where Michael recommended that we eat our picnic lunch.

The park was peaceful, with giant five to seven hundred year old copper beech, maple, and chestnut trees. Our elemental friends, who had been absent that morning—Christian sites and holy days not being a big draw for pagans—were wandering amongst the trees and also having picnics. My leprechaun colleague was seated under a gigantic oak with his feet up. He was drinking from an immense crock, which I could only hope contained tea, and not *poteen*.

Leprechauns are famous for brewing *poteen* (pronounced 'potcheen'), and my friend loved it nearly as much as mead and Guinness. Poteen is an incredibly powerful alcoholic drink, which country Irish distil illegally from barley or potatoes. It has a ton of uses, and in olden times farmers rubbed it on their hands to ease the pain of arthritis, lit their turf fires with it, and gave it to sheep to keep off the chill. You have to be careful to drink only poteen that has a clear bluish light, or else it could kill you, or make you blind. I have drunk poteen on one occasion, and it was much like vodka, with a kick that takes away your breath.

"Of course, it is tea," replied Lloyd, reading my mind as he upped the crock and downed the rest. "We've got some healin' to do for the Earth, it bein' a special day and all for you 'humans', so I wouldn't be havin' any poteen, would I?"

"Well, it might be a kind of communion for you elementals, instead of wine like Christians drink," I joked with him.

"Not being Christian, we don't celebrate Pentecost, as we've got right relations with the spirit every day of the year," he retorted, emphasizing the word 'Christian' with his nose in the air. "Do you think humans have got exclusive rights to the spirit?" he continued, querying me.

"Of course not," I answered.

"Right answer, lucky for you," he agreed and, continuing in his scholastic tone, said, "The spirit is the life in you, me, the trees, the rocks, and even things you humans can't see. Unlike you humans, elementals don't have to find the spirit, 'cos we are the spirit. It is us, and we are it. Humans are always lookin' outside themselves tryin' to find spirit, when it is always in 'em and in all things."

Waving his hand from one side of the park to the other, my friend asked, "What do you see?"

In answer to his question I observed what the elementals were doing. Peggy's brownie, seated in the middle of a bunch of gnomes and fellow brownies, was taking tiny nibbles from a large slice of soda bread on which jam was slathered. Brownies are very fastidious and, maintaining proper decorum, she had tucked her long skirt tidily under her legs, and carefully picked up any crumbs that fell on her clothes. Feeling my eyes on her, the little sweetie looked up and gave me a bright smile, pleased to be noticed.

In contrast to the well-behaved brownies, Molly's goblin had gathered up all the bored 'young un's', who were mostly of leprechaun and goblin stock. He was leading them in a game of catch through Ute and Wolfgang and the older German pilgrims, who were seated quietly at a table attempting to eat their picnic in peace. Noticing my firm stare, the goblin gave me a mock bow, reminiscent of a jester's, and sauntered away, whistling jauntily, showing that he, too, could behave.

Meanwhile, the two teenage trolls, leaning against a tree, stuffed their mouths with gigantic thighs from what might have been a sheep. Although the leprechaun and many elementals are vegetarian, trolls are serious carnivores. They are usually loners and the fact that they had joined a group of humans and other elementals, dedicated to working together, testified to how successful my leprechaun crony had been in his work.

"I was not talking about my folks, Silly," said my friend, amused at my perception of his fellow elementals. "I meant you to tell me, what do you see, when you look at the trees?"

"If I look with my inner sight, I see the branches and leaves of the trees absorbing energy from light. The light moves down through the trunk and through its roots, deep down into the earth. Then, the energy moves up the same way, feeding the tree and extending vitality through a large radius to all beings in the vicinity. A conscious being, a *deva*, assists with this process," I responded, saving the most important point until last.

"What do you mean by the word *deva*?" Lloyd asked, as if I were taking his exam.

"Deva comes from the Sanskrit word meaning god, celestial being, or angel," I answered him in a like manner. "In the ancient Vedas of India, stemming back three thousand years, devas were known to look after the forces of nature and the elements of earth, air, fire, and water. Celtic and Hindu traditions have a common Indo-European origin and many of their beliefs are similar.'"

"Are these devas elementals?"

"I'd say so, but not like you," I responded. "Leprechauns, elves, gnomes, trolls, and other earth elementals are more solid and individualized than devas. You're more like humans. Devas are very different."

"Describe how they are different," he interjected, peering at me over his bifocals and continuing my test.

"To me, devas are more ethereal, more like moving waves of coloured conscious energy," I answered the 'professor.' "I've seen devas growing trees, forests, and even great mountain ranges. They not only *know*, but *are* the divine plan, and devas grow everything in the natural world according to this plan. The tree devas in this park are as large as their trees and quite evolved."

"Well done, you pass," said the elemental scholar enthusiastically, clapping me on the shoulder, as he leapt to his feet and darted off across the park.

"Bring yer folks to the far end under that old tree," he called back and pointed in the direction he wanted us to go. "That's the place that needs healin.'"

I waved my hand to get everybody's attention, and pointed them towards the tree that he had indicated. The location would not have been my first choice, as it was not private. The tree was situated next to a public path where locals could walk by and watch us. However, I trusted the leprechaun's reasons for choosing that location, and we formed a circle beside the old tree.

Gnomes, trolls, brownies, and our various other elemental partners followed Lloyd's lead and encircled the humans. Nor were we alone. Throughout the park, the devas of the trees focused their attention on us. The devas, like the elementals, intended to work with us humans to heal the Earth. My leprechaun co-leader wanted me to lead the prayers, so I accommodated him. I gave each human a candle to light and, as we did so, candles in the hands of the elementals also burst into flame. Our three races together envisioned all land, air, and water creatures living in peace, and I felt the Holy Spirit strengthen our prayers.

When we had finished, Robin, one of our pilgrims from Virginia who, like Caitlin, is an elemental hybrid, asked if she could say a few words. Robin has short hair and sparkling eyes framed by granny glasses set in a pixyish face. She, like many elemental hybrids, does not look her age and has an enthusiastic good humour that is contagious. Unlike some elemental hybrids who experience difficulty in managing in the world, Robin, being a brownie elemental, is an efficient business consultant in her day-to-day life.

Respecting her intuition, I gave her the go ahead and she led us in a prayer for the trees in the park. Her prayers completed, the elementals and humans disbanded and I sauntered back to the bus.

Michael, who had been watching the ceremony from the safety of the bus, addressed me. Pointing back towards the tree under which we had prayed he said, "It's interesting that you went to that tree."

"Why is that?" I asked.

"A famous criminal, a highwayman, was hanged from it." Michael answered, pleased to share a piece of information that he was sure I lacked.

"Indeed," I replied, better understanding why the leprechaun had wanted us to pray at that location. It was to erase the traumatic memory from that tree and the park, and I could only hope our prayers had succeeded.

It was only a short drive from Belcoo to Boa Island to see the two thousand year old 'Janus' statue in a pagan graveyard. Walking down an overgrown path, we passed through a turnstile located amidst a patch of stinging nettles. The double-sided pagan figure, about four feet high, stood inside the fenced-off area. The Janus statue is thought to be male on one side and female on the other and, as its hands rest in its private parts, the figure might once have been a fertility object. The graveyard was a desolate place because suicides and the non-baptised were buried here. Our elemental friends, not liking graveyards, even if they were pagan, had not joined us.

Janus Statue

"Very Irish," I thought, "to put suicides, who are unacceptable to the church, in the keeping of a pagan god."

Irish Catholics, one could argue, are still half-pagan, and fit their religion to practicality. For example, in Keel they attend Mass on Saturday evening, so they won't have to get up early on Sunday morning after a night of drinking at the pub. Very sensible!

"You'd best not linger," my elemental colleague interrupted my thoughts. "Some of yer folks want to go shoppin'. Sure, there could be a mutiny if you don't give it to 'em."

"If they mutiny," I replied to his suggestion, "lack of shopping will be way down their list, after microphones not working in the boat, Belfast, and lack of promised sites. You get the picture."

At the same time, I realized that he had a good point. Many in our group wanted to visit the Belleek factory to purchase the famous porcelain. I have discovered over the years that even 'spiritual' people like to shop, and so I always include some time for this. Fortunately, Paddy, efficient as always, drove us back in plenty of time.

Dinner was not up to the high standard of Mary's cooking the previous evening at the Unicorn. There were many downcast faces, which even shopping had not alleviated. I observed a growing sadness and frustration in the group. This in turn increased my anxiety that I could not help them. We were fast sinking into the next stage of dying, which, you will remember, is depression.

A lifetime pattern for me is the desire to satisfy people's needs and I couldn't. I yearned to share the magic and mystery of Ireland at its best, and what we were experiencing was its worst. Yes, I could be philosophical and say that the 'worst' was really the heart of the pilgrimage and the grist for our personal transformation. However, for a human being, it was the pits. I was being taken, as we all were, into my weakest areas.

The Big Three sat apart as usual and went to other accommodation before the rest of us had finished eating. I was surprised that they were lodging elsewhere, and could not reach them to review the next day's itinerary. Although I attempted to take the leprechaun's advice about living in the present moment, and tried to let go of my expectations of receiving positive experiences, I was uneasy when I retired for the night.

chapter eight

the worst day

From the moment I opened my eyes the next morning, I had a premonition that it would not be a good day. I already knew that we would miss two of the three sites on the original itinerary because they were closed. These were the Ulster History Park, which had full-scale habitations from the Stone Age to the seventeenth century, and Emain Macha, a Bronze Age fort known as the Irish Camelot.

The third site planned, and the only one remaining, was Beaghmore Stone Circle. I had visited Beaghmore—also called the Dragon's Teeth—the last time I'd brought a group to Ireland and was certain our folks would enjoy it. Also, it was pagan, so I thought that my leprechaun pal would want us to go there.

As people packed up their gear, I went over to Michael and Paddy's table to review the day's itinerary. Brian had already left for Belfast where we would be staying that night. Brian's very absence should have told me that we were about to descend to new lows, as he was never and I mean *never*-around to solve these difficult situations.

"Beaghmore is too far out of our way, if we have to get to Belfast tonight," said Paddy, studying the map.

"But Paddy," I countered. "We have to give the people something they've been promised."

"Also, it's on a small road, and I don't think the bus can make it," Paddy responded, returning to his favourite reason for saying 'no,' as he, and not I, had the final say in what the bus could and could not do.

Michael, who had been silently seething, erupted, "This is the worst organized tour I've ever been on, and I'm thinking of packin' it in."

Paddy nodded sagely in agreement.

I felt that they, and Michael especially, held me responsible for the situation in which they found themselves. It would have been a stretch for them to believe that Brian and James the Lep, two Irish men who had been in the business for seven years, could have created this mess. In their shoes, I would have had a hard time believing it as well.

The three of us were continually facing unknown situations, which in turn raised fears, frustration, and now anger. When we cannot solve our problems, as we were not able to do, then we need to accept 'what is', and do this with as much grace and compassion for each other as possible. I knew this was the only option open to us.

Leaning forward and appealing to their better selves, I entreated, "Michael, we are all in the same boat here. I know it's hard for you to do a professional job, as it is for Paddy, and as it is for me, too. However, we have to be as professional as we can be, given the circumstances."

I could feel that Paddy and Michael were not budging on Beaghmore and, because we needed a guide and bus driver more than a site, I conceded. "If we don't go to Beaghmore, what could we offer the group?"

They must have already worked out a plan, because Michael responded all too quickly with, "I know a deserted village right on our way and we could go there."

Paddy hastily nodded his assent.

I was not pleased with the suggestion. However, insisting on Beaghmore would be disastrous. "All right," I accepted. "What can we see in Armagh, since we can't visit Emain Macha?"

"I could take them to St. Patrick's Cathedral," Michael offered, warming to his own suggestion.

"I'd best get me bus," Paddy said, jumping up from the table.

The catastrophe had been averted, at least for the time being, but I was left shaken by our discussion. I felt caught in the middle, unable to satisfy either the needs of our group, or to build a good working rapport with Paddy, Michael, and Brian. Some friends and colleagues of mine were on the tour, but they had come for a good time, and I didn't want to burden them with my problems.

One of these was Ruth, who was also the manager of our institute in Canada. This was the longest holiday that she and her hard-working husband, Ralph, had ever taken in their lives and, although I knew she would be sympathetic to my plight, I wanted them to have a worry-free holiday. Also, I could tell, by looking at averted eyes and down-turned mouths, that some group members were not convinced of the deeper spiritual significance of our difficulties and might even think that I was somehow responsible.

I was only too aware that our beleaguered pilgrims were not receiving the great holiday in Ireland for which they had paid. It is much easier for me to roll with 'what is' when I am the only person affected. I find it much more difficult when others are involved. If there is such a thing as being overly responsible, I have a bad case of it, and the tour was ripping this quality out of me piece by painful piece.

Our folks were waiting to depart as I came out of the meeting. Ruth must have noticed my distress, as she asked, "Are you all right?"

"Just more Craic," I smiled cryptically, and hastily rushed to my room, grabbed my backpack, and left. We drove in silence that morning and everyone, like myself, appeared to be feeling either despondent or angry. On a usual tour, folks would be chatting, joking, and sharing their experiences. The silence that day was deafening.

Even the leprechaun and his cronies were absent, as we besieged pilgrims journeyed into the darker and darker areas of the Craic.

After about two hours of driving, Michael started giving Paddy directions to the deserted village. I would never have imagined that things could get worse, but they did. Soon we were lost, wandering up and down back roads. After much confusion, I hazarded a suggestion that we ask the next person we saw for directions and, to my surprise, Paddy took me up on it. As we drove around yet another hairpin turn, we saw a man coming out of a bungalow. You should have seen the man's astonished look as a fifty-seater bus full of tourists swerved into his driveway.

Paddy, leaning out his window, asked for directions. The man seemed to know where the deserted village was, as a lot of right and left-hand gestures accompanied his words. Michael kept silent during the instructions. Reversing the bus, Paddy soon had us on our way and we found the village without further difficulty. The immediate problem was that there were no toilets; so, before doing anything else, thirty people set out urgently in search of bushes.

Reconvening, Michael did his best to give us a tour of the deserted village. Unfortunately, the expression, "you can't make a silk purse out of a sow's ear," sums up our experience. The village was terrible. There was absolutely nothing to see, and people began to complain actively that they weren't receiving what they'd signed up for. Everyone unanimously agreed that they were not pleased to be going to Belfast that night. I could only hope that St. Patrick's Cathedral in Armagh would be interesting. Packing back into the bus, we set out for Armagh. Once again we drove in silence as neither Michael nor I had anything positive to say.

"He's one of us, so to speak," my leprechaun friend said, appearing on the seat across the aisle and nodding in Michael's direction.

"You mean Michael is an elemental?" I asked incredulously.

"No, but he's got giant's blood," he replied, before adding. "That's part of the problem why you two aren't gettin' on."

I had actually suspected that Michael might have been a hybrid with giant heritage, so Lloyd's words merely confirmed my existing thought. As I got on so well with elemental, angelic, and other hybrids, I didn't understand why Michael and I could not get on.

"On no account does *that* one want to know *that* part of himself," sighed my friend, stressing the word 'that' twice. "It's very sad when beins' don't want to know their true nature. This is why he has studied giants, spirits, and 'the little people' his whole life. They fascinate him, but he wants to keep them at arm's length, safe and all. Then, along you come with thirty folks believin' in these 'mythic' beins' and he finds himself in the middle of a deep sea. This is why he never takes part in any of yer meditations, or listens to what you've got to say. It's all too close for comfort."

"What can I do?" I asked, wanting to forge a better relationship with Michael.

"Absolutely nothin'," my amused pal chortled. "You humans always want to make everythin' nice. Just learn to accept what is."

"Would it hurt, if I asked him to talk about giants, in theory of course?"

"Naw. That one loves to expound, don't he?" the leprechaun laughed, not recognizing himself in his words.

Leaning forward to get Michael's attention, I asked him to tell us about giants. He perked up at the suggestion, as he found pleasure in sharing, and knew that we enjoyed listening to him.

Turning on the microphone, he started. "Tanis has asked me to speak of giants and there's quite a history. In the Bible there was Goliath who was killed by David, and in Genesis we read about the *Nethalim*, who were said to be the sons of the gods and mortals destroyed during the great flood. We've even got giants in Ireland and Finn MacCool, our legendary hero and Knight of the Red Branch, was said to be a giant. As a point of interest, the Knights of the Red Branch are the Irish equivalent to the Knights of the Round Table of King Arthur's Camelot."

Spectacles appeared on the leprechaun's nose, and he made a great show of getting out his scorecard.

"In northern Antrim," Michael continued with enthusiasm, "ancient seamen were warned to stay away from Portrush and Ballycastle for fear of the cannibalistic giants who lived there. In fact, three skulls were found in the 1800s that were three times the size of those of normal men."

"It's true," I couldn't help but notice, "Michael does have a rather large head."

"Outside of Portrush in Antrim," Michael said, "it's recorded in the ordinance survey that in 1834 a gigantic skull was found in the ground of Ballywillan Church. It was reburied by the priest who re-consecrated the ground, as the skull was pagan."

Gazing at my friend's scorecard I noticed that, for once, Michael was getting all green check marks.

Michael continued, "There are large women in Antrim even in modern times and Mary Murphy, our most famous giantess at seven feet tall, comes from Portrush. She was presented to King William the Third and Mary the Second in 1691. Mary was very beautiful and many men proposed marriage, but she accepted a French sea captain. He gave up the sea and started exhibiting her in a sideshow. Mary was last heard of in 1710 when she was an alcoholic, deserted by her husband, living outside Paris."

With these last words Michael turned off the microphone, signalling the end of the talk.

"No wonder Michael doesn't want to admit, even to himself, that he's got giant's blood," I thought sympathetically.

"Very true," Lloyd agreed sadly. "There's why elementals and giants are alike. Most humans don't have much use for either of us, do they?"

I was on the point of responding to his statement, when I noticed that we were entering Armagh, one of Ireland's oldest cities. Paddy, being a boy from the south, didn't know Armagh. Why should we be surprised, therefore, when we found ourselves in the middle of the city going downhill the wrong way on a one-way street? Paddy immediately saw his error, came to a stop, and attempted to reverse the bus, only to discover that cars were behind him and that we were blocking a four-way intersection.

"Michael, git out and help me reverse the bus!" Paddy exclaimed, swinging open the door.

Michael hopped off, but appeared not to know what to do. From the bus windows thirty pairs of eyes watched him go into a neighbouring shop. To get help, I guessed, but he did not reappear.

Paddy, in an agitated state, erupted, "What the heck is he doin'?"

Waves of uncertainty, climbing closer to hysteria, rumbled throughout the bus.

When Michael still did not return, my elemental co-leader dug me in the ribs and urged, "What are you waitin' for, ask Yer Man if you can help."

I was reluctant to do so, as I might be meddling in 'man's business', but my insistent friend wouldn't let up and kept digging me in the ribs.

I bent forward and tentatively asked Paddy, "Would you like me to help?"

"Would you, please?" he answered gratefully.

Disembarking, I discovered that our problem was more serious than it had looked from my safe seat inside. The bus had totally blocked traffic on four sides.

"What am I doing, letting 'that' leprechaun talk me into trying to fix this mess?" I thought to myself, as I've never directed traffic in my life.

Looking up, I saw concerned pilgrims peering at me from the windows. Frowns had set on some of their faces, although many were laughing merrily and, truth be told, had caught the spirit of the Craic. Dr. Carl and Peggy had out their cameras and were taking pictures for posterity; Katje, in her calm, gracious style, was waving at me and smiling. And the leprechaun…? Dressed in a miniature version of a traffic cop's uniform, my pal was holding up a red stop sign, blowing a whistle, and generally having a wonderful time laughing at the situation.

Taking a clue from his antics and remembering how I'd seen traffic police do it, I dove into the unfamiliar role. Raising my left hand, I stopped one lane from moving, while directing another lane through the intersection. The looks on the faces of the drivers were something to behold. When was the last time they would have seen a female tourist in lime green Capri pants, sandals, and sunhat hop off a bus to direct traffic on a congested street? I'm sure that the answer was 'never.' Finally, I was able to clear enough space for Paddy to back up. He turned the bus into a through road, swung open the door, and I climbed on.

"Well done," he said gratefully, while I was greeted by applause from those who had witnessed the fiasco. Lloyd, grabbing his belly, rolled around in his seat, howling with joy.

A few moments later, Michael reappeared and got on the bus. In silent accord, none of us commented.

"On no account say anythin'," my elemental chum whispered. "Giants be proud and touchy."

Paddy parked the bus and Michael suggested that we meet after lunch for a cathedral tour. At the agreed-upon time some folks appeared, but others continued shopping. They didn't miss much. The cathedral is a not very interesting nineteenth-century building.

It was a despondent group that set out for Belfast later that afternoon. It would be a long drive to see nothing—and I mean *nothing*—and then we would have to retrace our steps south the next day. Brian claimed that it was necessary to overnight in Belfast because James had been unable to find accommodation in Armagh. I thought his explanation weak, but it was difficult to know where the truth lay.

Half an hour outside Belfast, Michael turned on the microphone and commenced telling us about the difficulties between the Protestants and Catholics. He mentioned that he was a Protestant married to a Catholic and that his life had been threatened more than once. Michael's words were to be taken seriously as, living in Belfast, he knew the ins and outs of the political situation. He strongly suggested that we remain in our hotel that evening as it was unsafe to go out.

"Just the other week," he recounted, "a tourist was killed because he wandered into the wrong section of Belfast."

The day was ending as badly as it had started. I racked my brain trying to think of what I could do to redeem a very unpleasant situation. A group meditation on peace seemed the obvious choice for the evening.

The only good thing I could say about the hotel in Belfast was that the beds were comfortable and the showers hot. The dinner was a disgrace and reminded me of food in university dorms. Slimy-looking Irish stew and pasta were our two choices, topped off with store-bought cake for dessert. This disagreeable dinner was delivered in a cafeteria-style line in the middle of the main foyer of the hotel. Unappetizing food, accompanied by terrible surroundings, in a violent town, did not make for well-satisfied people.

To make matters worse, unpacking my suitcase to get ready for our meeting, I discovered that, in the morning's brouhaha with Paddy and Michael, I had left my wash-up bag and some clothes back at the last hotel. I phoned James the Lep and he promised to have my belongings couriered to Dublin by the next night. Blessed are those who believe!

Meanwhile, I was able to borrow toothpaste from Katje, a toothbrush from Peggy, contact lens solution from Diana, and a comb from Melanie. I had neither lipstick nor eyeliner, so I resigned myself to being totally makeup-less—which leaves some women, me included, feeling a bit naked. I already felt stripped by the events of the pilgrimage. Little did I know that evening that I would soon be thrown into an even deeper abyss.

A discontented group met for a meditation for peace and several people, including Kirsten and Diana, ignoring Michael's advice, went in search of music and drink—probably lots of drink. Nor did I blame them. I would have liked a drink or two, myself. Many were having a miserable time and were not sure where to lay the blame or, like me, how to correct the situation. They were not speaking with me directly, but I could tell by downcast faces that they were unhappy. Also, with the Big Three keeping themselves apart from us, our folks felt unwelcome in a country renowned for hospitality and warmth.

I continued to correct what I could, sensed the inner purpose of our difficulties, and had a growing acceptance of the Craic. However, as my leprechaun friend had pointed out earlier, all of us needed to let go of what we wanted and to surrender even more deeply to 'what is.' With this goal in mind, I began the meditation session. My leprechaun co-leader plopped into the seat beside me to, hopefully, lend a hand.

"Let's go around the room and choose angel cards to help us understand what we are experiencing," I suggested, framing our situation optimistically, but at the same time realistically.

I was relieved and grateful to hear our lovely older women Hannah and Sara speaking of the tour in positive terms. Robin and Katje, willing to give the elementals the benefit of the doubt, also spoke of many things they were learning from them. Melanie, always supportive, smiled encouragingly at me, while her husband Max, bless his heart, kept his temper and attempted to keep an open mind. Lloyd, I saw out of the corner of my eye, smiled warmly at them, nodding in approval.

Other people remained sullen and, although not voicing their complaints loudly, they had obviously not accepted the leprechaun's teachings. My elemental co-leader watched them closely, and I could see him making mental notes about what he and his friends could do to nudge them along.

Picking up on my concern for the pain that others might experience, he said, "The time will never be as good as now with so many folks, in the same place, believin' in us. So why miss the opportunity to do 'em a good turn?"

"Good doesn't necessarily mean happy, or joyful, or any of those nice feelings that we're overdue to experience, does it?" I asked, on behalf of our oppressed pilgrims.

"We elementals are about doin' things in the quickest way possible. You know that. And we're makin' 'reeeemarkable' progress with you humans," he smiled widely, congratulating himself.

"Are you saying that the sooner we humans are able to accept 'what is', the sooner we'll be flowing with the Craic?" I asked.

"I couldn't have said it better meself," he smirked, giving me a friendly punch in the shoulder.

"Buddhist's would say acceptance of 'what is' is the key to inner peace," I elaborated, mentally clapping him on the shoulder, as guys love to do when they're bonding.

"The Dalai and I see eye to eye," replied the leprechaun, changing his normal attire to that of a Buddhist monk, robed in flowing orange and maroon cloth from which his large boots protruded. This was obviously his signal to move on to the next part of the evening—our meditation for peace.

Turning to our group, I commented, "The Dalai Lama has said that, until people go through their own transformation, there will never be peace in the world. Inner and outer peace has become a major theme of our pilgrimage. It is perfect that we have been brought, however unwillingly, to Belfast with its history of violence. Letting go of all expectations and maintaining a sense of welcoming acceptance of 'what is' is the key to inner peace. Our elemental friends are wonderful teachers of this, even if it feels as if we are engaged in a crash course."

As our meditation started, I looked out of the corner of my eyes at my leprechaun colleague. He had crossed his legs in a meditative position on his chair and was rolling his half-closed eyes towards the heavens with an exaggerated look of beneficence on his face. He was obviously enjoying his new role as the first-ever leprechaun convert to Buddhism. His top hat had been replaced by a pyramid-shaped hat resembling one I'd seen on 'The Dalai', except that the leprechaun's hat was complete with green shamrocks. How could I not smile as I, in my own way, meditated for peace?

I only wished—for perhaps the hundredth time—that others could see and hear the leprechaun as I did. It gave me an advantage in understanding the inner purpose of the often-difficult situations that we encountered, as well as enjoying his over-the-top sense of humour.

During my meditation I reflected on how the pilgrimage had given me ample opportunity to observe what helps people, myself included, to move into non-attachment and acceptance of what the universe, in the form of the Craic, gives us.

First, I noticed that we accept difficult situations more easily when we are not heavily invested in the outcome. Second, if we trust some-one, as many did me, or as I did the leprechaun, we have greater faith in what that one says. Third, it helps move us to acceptance when we hear the same message from more than one source. In many ways, I felt like a voice crying in the wilderness for the Big Three did not sup-port my perception of reality.

"Wouldn't it be nice," I thought to myself, ending the meditation and opening my eyes, "if there were someone, other than myself, to help our folks to understand the deeper inner lessons of what is transpiring?"

"Yer wish, me dear, is soon to be granted," said my leprechaun chum, tipping his pyramid hat to me in a way that Buddhists might have found sacrilegious. "We elementals see that you and yer 'humans' need a bit of a break from the dark Craic and are goin' to give you some lessons from the light Craic."

With that cryptic—Thank the powers that be!—hopeful message, he disappeared.

Chapter Nine

The Craic

Lovely sun welcomed us the next day as it had on every day thus far. "Be grateful for that," I thought, preparing for our departure. Today we were heading south, back to Dublin. It was a long drive on the bus, although we were fortunate to have three sites to visit en route. Sing out the hallelujahs! At long last our pilgrims, by some miracle, would receive what they had been promised.

Our first stop was to pick up Dr. Tim Campbell, the Director of St. Patrick's Heritage Centre in Downpatrick, who was going to accompany us personally on a tour. Tim was a pleasant young man and Michael relinquished his guide's seat so that Tim could sit down to speak with us. Downpatrick is Northern Ireland's administrative centre and, unlike Belfast, it is an old coastal town. There are many sites around Downpatrick related to St. Patrick, and one of them is Struell Wells (*struell* meaning *stream*).

Arriving at Struell Wells, we were greeted by a tall, white-bearded man who looked to be a cross between a scholar and a hippie. "This is Dr. Stan Papenfus," said Tim, introducing his friend. "Stan is a psychologist with an interest in healing waters and sacred sites and he'll show you about."

"Struell Wells is abandoned now, but it has had a two thousand year history that peaked during the seventeenth century when people flocked to its curative waters to heal themselves, especially their eyes," said Stan, commencing our tour.

Struell Wells

Stan guided us to each of the baths and explained their purpose. Caitlin descended into one to splash water on her slowly healing face, while Molly rolled up her sleeve and cupped water onto her hurt arm. All of us took turns putting water on our various injuries and sore bits, while Stan looked patiently on. Many, like Dr. Carl and Wolfgang, filled bottles with healing water to use back home in healing preparations and rituals.

We enjoyed the beautiful, peaceful setting and I thought the visit to Struell Wells had ended when Stan, glancing at me with a mischievous twinkle in his eye, offered to read from his book called *Paddy's Chin*. At first I hesitated, as I wanted to allow time to visit Tim's centre in

Downpatrick. There, we could see a film on St. Patrick, eat lunch, and visit the much-needed toilets. Just as I was on the point of begging off, the leprechaun popped up behind Stan and, peeking around his shoulder—or should I say, waist—exclaimed, "Say yes, say yes! I've been days settin' this up." At that moment, a large sign with neon words flashing 'Light Craic' appeared above Stan's unsuspecting head.

"That would be lovely," I accepted, trying to keep from laughing at the leprechaun's neon sign, while signalling our folks to join us near a ruined building. Enjoying the warm sun, we seated ourselves amidst the wildflowers and, as if by magic, elementals manifested, excited for the story to begin. The teenage trolls leaned against the crumbling building thumping each other on the shoulder in anticipation, while Peggy's brownie, Little Sweetie, as I referred to her, sat next to Peggy grinning from ear to ear.

Molly's goblin, hyperactive as always, but attempting to sit still, fidgeted with pieces of grass. I must admit he had grown on me and I had warmed to him as a reformed criminal trying to go straight. Hearing my thought, the clever goblin, the quickest of all elementals, shot me a half-smile and said, "Yer not half bad yerself ... for a human."

Wow! A compliment...from a goblin. Suddenly, I recalled the pictures of the happy elementals and humans sitting together in the grass, which had dropped out of the leprechaun's portfolio in the bedroom in Keel. Now, we were living it. Thank heavens, that scene had been a happy one.

With the impeccable timing of a good storyteller, Stan waited for our attention. Finding it, he commenced. "My book is an Irish rendition of the Tao Te Ching and the Tao is what the Irish call the Craic. The Craic, like the Tao, means *enlightened banter*, and the process of experiencing, expressing, and exploring reality. You will never understand Ireland, or the Irish, if you don't understand and enjoy the Craic."

Looking down at his book, he opened it lovingly and started

reading. "A truly wise person, Your Man, lives in the heart of events, goes with the flow, takes things as they come, is cute as a fox, and just keeps cracking away, despite all obstacles. 'Obstacles? What obstacles?' says Your Man, 'Sure it's all good Craic, powerful Craic.'"

"My god," I thought to myself. "Stan could have been on our pilgrimage." Gazing at the others, I noticed they were all smiling in accord. Humour obviously qualified as light Craic to my leprechaun friend.

Stan resumed his reading. "There is nothing for it, then, but to go with the flow of the Craic…'Not to follow the way of the Craic is to make a complete eejit of yourself,' says Your Man."

By now, Molly's goblin and many youngish gnomes were rolling around on the grass and laughing, while the tiny faeries, accompanying Ute and Wolfgang, hopped from flower to flower twittering in pleasure.

"You see what great Craic we've been havin' with you folks?" said the leprechaun, chuckling.

Stan looked up and, wanting to make sure that we understood what the Craic meant, pulled a few well-known phrases out of their original context. For this, I'm sure the Craic will absolve him.

Stan quoted, "Albert Einstein said, 'Everything is relative,' meaning relative to the Craic. Also, William Shakespeare wrote, 'To be or not to be.' Being caught between the two is the Craic."

By this time we humans, like the elementals, were laughing at Stan's references.

Lowering his eyes, Stan continued reading. "'Just going for a dander,' says Your Man. His needs met, his food enjoyed, he wants no more from the world. That's why the Craic just pours out of him."

Stan paused after each little gem, allowing them to sink in. I could feel his words healing the difficulties that some of the folks had been having with the Craic. You could see them reflecting in a positive way.

Stan resumed. "The Craic shows you what you're really like. No speculation required. Flattery misleads. Insults kill the spirit. What are you saving yourself for? The reason you can't beat the Craic is because it's on your side."

Dr. Carl's reserved elf, standing beside Kirsten's gorgeous female elf, gave Stan a nod of approval indicating that Stan had passed the storyteller's test. The elementals looked joyfully, albeit smugly, at their human partners, and I witnessed their pride in their wonderful ability to work with the Craic to teach us.

What the Irish call the Craic is the crack between the world of the humans and the elementals, between what we want and what we have. It is the place where chaos reigns but, as science has lately discovered, chaos has its own order. We had been having the Craic for the majority of our pilgrimage.

"Some unplanned events, such as Stan's' readin' here, work out excellently, don't they?" my leprechaun co-leader asked me, waiting for applause.

"Absolutely," I said, giving him his due. "It's not the surprises, but the ratio between sad and happy surprises, which could use a bit of rebalancing."

"Don't you 'humans' have an expression, "Spare the rod and spoil the child?'"

"We have another expression, "A little bit of honey makes the medicine go down," I said in response, thinking that my fellow pilgrims and I were overdue for the honey.

I was grateful for Stan's reading and too soon our time with him ended. His Irish translation of the Tao had deepened our understanding of the Craic as a path to becoming more conscious. This was, after all, the purpose of pilgrimage. A much lighter and more accepting mood surrounded us as we headed back to Downpatrick to visit the toilets—by now urgently required—and to have lunch.

"You humans with your fascination with the loo," commented my elemental friend. "You'd think bushes would do fine for most things."

I was positive that I wouldn't be able to convert our folks to using the bushes, but I was intrigued by what elementals did with their, should I say, private waste.

"Is that what you use?" I asked curious.

"Of course we do. That way all the goodness goes back into the earth. Much better conservation, you know?" he said, nudging me.

"Do your females also use the bushes?"

"For most things," said Lloyd, shifting uncomfortably now that I'd entered the personal topic of females.

"And for other things?"

"For those other things we have holes in the ground, just like sensible humans used to do," he replied, as if he were talking to an 'eejit.'

Just then, we pulled into St. Patrick's Centre and many of us rushed for the toilets. We had time to squeeze in the film about St. Patrick before loading on the bus to drive south to Monasterboice.

Monasterboice High Cross

Monasterboice is famous for its ninth-century high crosses with biblical scenes. Michael resumed his guiding, which he did well when he was on familiar ground, and our folks walked around taking pictures. As Monasterboice is a Christian site, the elementals were absent and might have still been enjoying themselves at the wells.

I, on the other hand, was feeling sick and remained with Paddy as he washed his bus. We were only a few hours drive from Dublin; so Paddy was doing his own version of a ritual cleansing before going home. Professional driver that he was, Paddy had finished by the time the group was ready to leave for Dublin, which would be our home for the remaining four nights.

I became increasingly ill and remember little about the drive. Checking into the hotel, several people—who shall remain nameless—discovered that their rooms had only showers, not baths. Annoyed, they asked for their rooms to be changed. Although they understood the theory about the Craic, the slightest inconvenience made them forget. When we aren't happy we often get picky about little things which would not make a difference under normal circumstances.

Also, there can be two of us. One understands and agrees with the lessons of the Craic—the higher self who, as a neutral observer of events, can see the light and humour in an uncomfortable situation. The other part, the human part, may collapse under the burden of these same events. That was me. I received the last room down a gloomy corridor in the old section of the hotel. Opening the door, I squeezed through and discovered only enough room for a bed. The room was dark and overlooked the furnace fan on the roof, which made a continual noise like a helicopter taking off. Exhausted by the ordeal, Craic or no, I fell into bed.

PART II

INNER PILGRIMAGE BY BED

CHAPTER TEN

The Elves of Glendalough

I t was pouring rain when the alarm clock rang the next morning. Perhaps our sunny days were behind us. All night I had coughed and burned with fever and, exhausted, had not been able to throw off the virus. Picking up the clock, I shut it off and lay in bed reviewing my choices. Option one: get dressed and go to Glendalough, the site we were scheduled to visit that day. Option two: stay in bed and attempt to recover. My body needed to stay in bed; however, I loved Glendalough and had been looking forward to introducing our folks to the faery sites there.

"Great choice!" I said aloud, discovering to my surprise that I had lost my voice.

Amused by yet another experience of the Craic, I was startled when the leprechaun popped up beside me in bed. He was dressed in an old-fashioned nightshirt down to his ankles with a pointed nightcap on his head. A gigantic red scarf was wrapped around his neck, a thermometer hung out the side of his mouth, and his nose was inflamed, as if he'd been blowing it all night.

"I'm played out," he exclaimed, taking the thermometer from his mouth and wheezing, "Tryin' to order all you humans has done me in."

"Well, being 'ordered' by you has done me in, too," I rejoined, choking out the words in a whisper.

"We need a couple of days off to put up our feet and recover before the walkin' tour starts," replied my elemental chum, staying well clear of my complaint.

"I couldn't agree more," I groaned, thinking of the walking tour, which I was leading the day after the present pilgrimage had ended. I was very much looking forward to it, although not in my present condition.

"So, we're agreed," he responded, sinking lower in the bed and closing his eyes.

Before I could rest, unlike my elemental co-leader, I needed to make arrangements for the others and to ask for help. Hacking, I slowly pulled myself out of bed and got dressed. Entering the breakfast room, I went directly to Robin, my elemental-loving colleague.

"Robin, as you can see, I'm not well. Will you please lead the group meditation today?" I asked whispering, which was as loud as my voice would go.

"Of course," she replied, eager to help. "What do you want me to do?"

"You won't need to know the history of Glendalough because Michael will take care of that," I croaked. "But take them down the valley to the ruins of the old church, called St. Saviour's Priory, as there are elementals who will meet you there. It would be wonderful, if you could lead the others in a guided visualization to meet the elementals."

"I'd love to do that," Robin said enthusiastically.

"I know you'll do a terrific job. Please apologize to the others for my absence."

"I will. Don't worry, just get well," she consoled me.

Excusing myself, I went to the sideboard and poured two large glasses of apple juice to take back to my room. Carrying the juice, I slowly shuffled to the counter where we had checked in the previous day. A young Irish woman, wearing a name badge saying *Maureen*, glanced at the juice in fleeting disapproval, and, prompting me to speak, asked, "Yes?"

Leaning towards her so she could hear me, and covering my mouth so as not to contaminate her, I uttered hoarsely, "As you can hear, Maureen, I'm not well and will be in the hotel for another three days. Therefore, if you could move me to a brighter room away from the noisy fan, I'd appreciate it."

"I'll see what I can do," she commiserated. "We don't have anything available right now, but something might come up when people check out. I'll ring you later."

Mouthing my thanks, I climbed the stairs to my tiny, dark, and noisy room.

Happily, the leprechaun had vacated the premises, so I hung the *Do Not Disturb* sign on the door and, without removing my clothes, climbed back into bed.

Despite the coughing and increasingly sore throat, I fell asleep and was awakened at noon by the phone ringing.

"We've got you another room," said a voice I recognized as Maureen's. "Come and get your key when you're ready."

Downing both glasses of apple juice, I dragged myself downstairs, picked up the key, and found my new room. Good fortune had smiled on me. It was double the size of the former closet and had a large window overlooking the street, through which I viewed a great deal of water cascading to the ground.

"Oh, those poor people," I thought, reflecting on how exposed our folks would be in the wild Glendalough Valley. Sending them wishes of goodwill and grateful that I had decided to forgo the journey, I put on my nightie and returned to bed.

Snuggling under the covers, I had just closed my eyes when up popped a cheery voice. "Livin' the life of luxury," said the leprechaun, pulling me back from blessed oblivion.

Opening my eyes, I saw him perched comfortably at the foot of the bed and noted that he, at least, looked in better shape than he had that morning.

"We elementals have got great 'reeecuperative' powers," he stated, trying out an unfamiliar human word.

"I can see that," I croaked, smiling in spite of myself.

"Anyway, enough idle chatter. I've come to take you on an inner tour by bed, while the others continue on the outer tour by bus. You could say, we're havin' a bit of a *de*tour," he broke up, laughing at his own cleverness.

"I would say that quite a bit of the tour has been a *de*tour," I replied in kind. "I think I'd rather sleep."

"No, you wouldn't," he persisted, unwilling to let me be. "You can go to all the places the others are visitin' without ever leavin' yer bed. You can travel down the energy tracks, of what you humans love to call yer past memories, and have a much better time than those poor sods out in the rain."

Listening to his words, I glanced at the window and saw the rain beating down. I must admit the downpour made the leprechaun's offer sound inviting so, closing my eyes, I embarked on his suggestion. Memories of former visits to Glendalough immediately arose.

The first time I saw Glendalough was with Peter and Elizabeth Gill, two older Irish friends who had a healing centre outside Wicklow Town. It was a beautiful May Day almost twenty years ago when we drove through the mountains into the magical valley. An hour's drive south of Dublin, Glendalough is situated beside two lakes deep in the Wicklow Mountains National Park. St. Kevin established a monastery there in the sixth century that, in time, attracted thousands of students and teachers, making it renowned during the Dark Ages as a centre for learning and scholarship. The monastery finally ceased in the eighteenth century, some 1100 years after its founding.

St. Kevin's Church

Twenty years ago Glendalough, like so many present-day tourist destinations, remained relatively undiscovered. Peter, Elizabeth, and I were alone, as we meandered through the monastic ruins, looking at an excellent tenth-century round tower used four times to repel the Vikings, and the tiny, classic Irish stone church of St. Kevin dating from the same period. Early monastic ruins stretch for miles around the lakes, but the remains of a stone circle demonstrate that Glendalough was also a pre-Christian habitation.

"Move along to the elves," my pal commented, cutting into my reverie and losing patience with the speed at which humans reminisce. I hastened to comply.

When my friends went for lunch, I decided to wander deeper into the woodland. Bluebells and moss, caressed by dappled light falling through the oak trees, covered the forest floor. Walking the quiet path, I felt the presence of many elves witnessing my stroll, but they remained unseen.

Individuals often feel something or someone watching them. It could be an animal, elemental, a person, or even a ghost. Energy accompanies every thought and action, and you can feel that energy when a being turns its attention towards you. Some people describe this as, "The hair stood up on the back of my neck." It is possible to discount this feeling, as it is subtle and nothing is seen in the three-dimensional reality to verify that perception. Yet, when you acknowledge the reality of this subtle energy, other realms open to you.

Elementals, like wild animals, prefer to see rather than to be seen, as humans—they have discovered to their detriment—may be a danger to them. I never force another being to show itself, so I waited patiently to discover if the elementals in Glendalough wished to contact me. Meanwhile, I was heartened that elementals and humans had coexisted peacefully in that valley for so many thousands of years.

"Elves, elves, elves!" Lloyd the Grand emphasized, trying to get me back on the track he wished me to pursue. Refusing to be hurried, pulling his leg a little, I went slowly back to my remembrances.

I glimpsed a path on my left, leading through the trees to a ruin, and decided to take it. Wandering through shamrocks in bloom with dainty white flowers, I came to the ruins of a quaint church resting quietly in a sunlit meadow strewn with multicoloured wildflowers. Walking into this idyllic setting, I lay down amidst the flowers and closed my eyes. Instantly, I was removed from the present time and transported to an earlier one.

Although I have experienced it many times, it is difficult to describe in words what a shift in time feels like. By using a neutral wisp of a thought—almost a thought before a thought—I reverse the magnetic energy poles that keep us in this three-dimensional world. This allows me to go through a black hole, a tunnel in my third eye, to travel to other locations, as well as forward and backward in time. Elementals have no difficulty moving in space and time, and do so matter-of-factly. The leprechaun has informed me that this skill will become a mode of transportation for humans in the future. An evolved human, or elemental, can occasionally catapult someone else into another time. This happened to me in Glendalough.

"Praise the goddess, she's almost there," my leprechaun chum intoned in the background.

Opening my inner eyes, I was surprised to see several graceful male and female elves approaching. Of human height, although more slender with sharper facial features and slightly slanted eyes, elves look similar to humans. You can tell that elves are not human in the same way you recognize the difference between a dog and a wolf. The eyes of a wolf and an elemental look wild and something in their energy signature bespeaks difference.

Elves in Western European countries come in many guises. Woodland elves, for example, are usually the size of a small human, or even a bit smaller, and dress mostly in browns and greens. They live almost exclusively in old forests. On more recent trips to Glendalough I have met woodland elves, but the elves that I met this first time were of the ruling caste.

These royal elves had great beauty and moved with grace. The clothes they wore would have been in fashion in the human world a few hundred years ago. The females were gowned in flowing, floor-length, gossamer-thin dresses; the males had on leggings and high deerskin boots. Not only their dress, but also their regal bearing, set them apart from humans of the twenty-first century. They had a look of command, or privilege, about them.

"Welcome to our home," the elves greeted me telepathically.

I began to rise, but they signalled me to remain on the grass. I felt discourteous lying down while they stood over me and, hearing my every thought, they laughed. Their laughter rang all the notes of pure crystal and I commenced sinking into a stupor. When I attempted to remain conscious, the beautiful female touched me gently on the arm and said, "Do not resist, my dear. We mean you no harm and merely want to merge our energies with you."

"Why would you want to do that?" I requested, wanting to understand their purpose before giving my consent.

"Both of our races will benefit by exchanging our energies with you," the female elf answered. "We cannot do this with many humans because they are too dense, so their energy would damage us. However, your energy is light and compatible as you have journeyed to our realm in other lives. We wish to help elementals to remain in the world and we are fading. You will give us an energy transfusion so that we are able to stay."

"Will this damage me in any way?"

"It will not," she responded, smiling. "We have brought you to an earlier time, when the elves were stronger, so that we will not be damaged during this energy exchange either."

The elves awaited my consent and knew the instant when I agreed. The graceful female elf withdrew her delicate, long-fingered hand from my arm and stepped back. Simultaneously, an equally beautiful male stepped closer and smiled down at me.

"Will you exchange energies with me?" he asked, bowing to me slightly, requesting permission.

"Ah yes," I thought to myself. "Even between species the interchange of energy is done between males and females." Images of faery tales raced through my mind of humans consorting with elves, for what they thought to be a short time, only to return to their own world to discover that hundreds of years had passed.

"Do not concern yourself," the elf's laughter tinkled through my awareness, putting me at ease. "You will go to sleep and wake only a few minutes later in this same meadow and in your present time."

Descending the road to sleep, I heard their voices echoing in my mind. "Thank you friend. We will meet again."

When I awoke in the meadow, I looked at my watch and discovered that only a few minutes had gone by. The elves had departed and I lay refreshed amidst the fragrant wildflowers. Perhaps the colours and smells were brighter; I cannot say with certainty. The memory of my experience lingered, although I did not speak of it for many years. I write about this occurrence now to help people who have had similar encounters. Our life energy—including its physical, etheric, emotional, mental, and spiritual manifestations—is a gift of spirit. Unbidden, it mingles with the energy of others, whether we are aware of it or not. We can choose to give, or to withhold energy, and it is important to decide consciously how to use our energy.

Lying in my bed in the hotel room in Dublin, I smiled to myself, remembering the many trips I had enjoyed to magical Glendalough, where I had often encountered the elves on the same shamrock-strewn path and meadow.

"Do you remember the significance of the shamrock?" my elemental friend said, appearing at the foot of the bed holding a bunch as a peace offering for hurrying me along. I noted, not with a little envy, that he now appeared totally recovered from his illness.

"I know a little about shamrocks," I thought towards him, wondering if his shamrocks would be the four-leaf lucky kind, rather than the ordinary three-leaf clover.

"The four-petalled shamrock are the kind that elementals recognize as their symbol, as four leaves represent earth, air, fire, and water," he asserted. "If humans learned to balance these four elements, as we nature spirits do, they would have a lot more luck in their lives. Patrick did you no service when he hijacked our shamrock. He didn't even get it right when he used the three-petalled clover to teach the Irish about the Christian trinity."

"Personally, I'm fond of the trinity. However, I agree with you that the four-leaf shamrock is a perfect symbol for elementals. I could use a little luck right now," I ventured hoarsely, eyeing the shamrocks.

"You've always got it with me," he said, jumping up and putting the bouquet in my hand. "Get some rest and I'll see you tomorrow."

"One moment before you go. You appeared with shamrocks, just as I had been thinking of them..."

"Thinkin' of them, and of the elves in Glendalough, to be exact," said Lloyd, with an air of exaggerated patience at needing to explain everything to the human.

"I understand our telepathic rapport during my waking state, but I'm curious to know how you are able to read my mind when you are not with me, or I'm sleeping, or journeying through past memories?" I inquired, fascinated to notice that, even using telepathy, my throat was still sore.

"You humans erect barriers and categories where none exist. Whether you are awake, asleep, sending me thoughts, or just thinkin' them yerself, it is all the same. Every thought, feelin', or action leaves an energy footprint that elementals see, hear, and feel. Don't be pretendin' that you can't do this as well, 'cos I can read anythin' you try to hide," my leprechaun crony egged me on with a smile.

"I recognize these energy signatures on people, but it is nowhere as good as your ability. To be honest, I'm not sure how I do it and thought you could shed some light on the 'how,'" I responded.

"It's easier for elementals 'cos we live in a lighter frequency—the one humans call the etheric. Because thoughts exist in the etheric, we are able to see, hear, and feel them without effort. For us, it's as obvious as you humans being able to observe people's actions," he said, gazing with pity at the human in her weakened state.

"When humans think happy thoughts, they have a lighter frequency that develops their ability to read energy footprints on others," he concluded, crossing his arms in front of his chest signalling that, once again, he was finished.

"One more question before you go. Are you working with the elves in Glendalough, and what is their relationship with the serious, older elf who works with Dr. Carl?"

"That's two questions. Don't think I didn't notice," said the leprechaun, smirking that he had caught me. "The elf who partners Dr. Carl is a revered scholar in our world, and has worked for hundreds of years with many humans, especially historians, inventors, and healers. He, the elves you met in Glendalough, and I are part of the same group that works cooperatively with humans."

"Did you have anything to do with the elves in Glendalough exchanging their energy with mine—this energy co-fertilization?"

"Well, yes and no."

Glancing at me, and seeing that I was not about to be put off, he continued in the laborious way a parent would speak to a child. "You were the obvious candidate. After all, you were at their home in Glendalough. You have the right energy footprint, bein' pro-elemental and with a light energy, so it's natural that they would want to exchange energy with you. We don't have borin' meetings talkin' about these things like you humans; we just do what is the thing to do. And…that's the last question I'm answerin'," said Lloyd the Grand hastily, before disappearing.

Drained by our conversation, I fell asleep immediately and did not awaken until dinnertime. Although very sick, I decided to go down for dinner to see how Robin and the others had made out.

Caitlin greeted me as I entered the dining room. Her burnt face was still an ugly red with blisters but, uncomplaining, she started raving about the day. "Robin did a wonderful job," she exclaimed joyfully, "and we met elementals."

Looking around the room I noticed happy faces and much laughter, a sure sign that Caitlin's opinion was shared. At that moment, Robin came over to speak with me.

"Even though the rain did not let up," she chattered, in her quick little optimistic voice, so typical of her hybrid brownie lineage, "we were still able to stay outside and do the guided visualization at the river."

"Super," I croaked, my voice as bad as it had been that morning. "Thank you so much Robin. I can see that the folks really enjoyed it."

I was grateful that everyone had enjoyed a wonderful day—at long last—and yet I was sad not to have been a part of it. I sat down and ate a bowl of soup, but found it too great a strain on my throat to speak with anyone. Trying not to cough and spoil people's dinner, I excused myself and returned to my room. Once there, I undressed and got back into bed, all the while feeling sorry for myself.

About a half hour later, I heard a knock at the door. Dragging myself out of bed, I opened it to discover Dr. Carl holding a black medical bag. He followed me inside and started conducting a medical assessment.

"You are exhausted and your energy is very low," Dr. Carl asserted, pronouncing his diagnosis. "You need to stay in bed and recover; so don't come with us tomorrow."

I was relieved that his assessment concurred with my own. Smiling to myself, I mused that it was a good thing that the elves hadn't exchanged energy with me *that* day, as they might have ended up with the flu. Dr. Carl gave me an injection. Appreciative of both the medical treatment and his unspoken support, I no longer felt quite so isolated and fell asleep as he was showing himself out. My last waking thoughts were of how difficult it was for me to ask for help and how important it was that I had. Robin, Dr. Carl, and my leprechaun pal were all willing, even pleased, to be able to help me. A great lesson learned through sickness. By surrendering leadership and control and trusting others to lead the group, I was learning more than if I had been able to lead.

CHAPTER ELEVEN

TUATHA DÉ DANANN, HILL OF TARA, AND NEWGRANGE

I had not improved the next morning, making it necessary to ask, once again, for help. Thank the goddess, we can always depend on the Craic to repeat a lesson until we have learnt it. I called Ruth and asked if she could come to my room before leaving for Newgrange.

Ruth reminds me of a human Raggedy-Ann—someone to hold close for comfort when you're having a really bad day. Ruth is a solid woman, about five-foot-seven with a ready smile, kind eyes, and a mop of curly brown hair. She is super efficient, skills she brings to running our institute's office in Canada, and I knew that I could count on her.

Seeing me huddled under the covers in bed, Ruth gave me a big loving grin. "Poor sick puppy," she said and commenced laughing. I joined her, although racking coughs soon shut down my wheezing laugh.

"It doesn't look like I'm going anywhere today, Ruth," I gasped out between coughs. "If you could lead the meditation at Newgrange, I'd very much appreciate it. There will be a special guide for our folks with private time in the chamber."

"It sounds wonderful," she replied and queried, "Is there anything else you'd like me to do?"

"Don't worry about doing anything at the Hill of Tara, as Michael will guide it. Also, they have an interpretive centre for the folks to visit," I replied.

Nodding her agreement, Ruth embraced me and walked out the door, leaving me the luxury of doing nothing but 'enjoying' the Craic.

"I should hope so," the leprechaun said, materializing at the foot of my bed. He was stretched out diagonally with legs crossed at the ankles, hands linked behind his neck, and head propped up on a gigantic pillow. He wore the gaudy red scarf that I'd last seen him in the previous day. From the neck down he was dressed in his normal green jacket, cut-off brown trousers, and heavy woollen socks sporting darn repairs in rainbow colours. Considerately, he had not worn his clunky clogs on the bed.

"You hope what?" I croaked.

"That you enjoy the Craic, of course," he replied. "It's the only way. Look at how competent people, like Ruth, Robin, and Dr. Carl, want to help; so you don't have to do everythin' yerself."

"Yes," I concurred. "I'm certainly blessed having so many talented, helpful friends. I'm just sad not to share two of my favourite sites with the folks."

"But you don't have to miss 'em," Lloyd exclaimed cheerily, leaping off the bed and into the armchair. His short legs dangled half a foot from the floor. Looking at me over the top of his bifocals, and placing his hands on a generous tummy, he looked every bit a miniature psychologist.

"I'm goin' to take you on an inner tour by bed to re-experience yer past memories at Tara and Newgrange in the sacred Boyne Valley," the leprechaun counsellor spoke, lowering and slowing his voice in what he believed to be a 'meditative' delivery.

"I'd love to do that," I agreed, enjoying the thought of being taken care of.

"Close... yer... eyes," he commanded, exaggerating his hypnotic tone.

"Just... follow... my...directions," my friend's voice intoned in my ear.

I drifted into remembrance. The fertile Boyne Valley, one of the most sacred areas of Ireland, has been occupied for over 5000 years. A Bronze Age ring fort has existed at the top of the Hill of Tara since 2500 BCE. This location was the capital of the Tuatha Dé Danann, meaning *'people of the goddess Danu'*, who were the mythical faery rulers of Ireland.

"Startin' without me, I see!" exclaimed Lloyd, breaking into my thoughts and pulling me back to the room. My inner tour would have to wait. Why should I be surprised!

"It's all very well for you to be the expert in human history, however, I'd like to say somethin' about elemental history, as both of our histories meet on the Hill of Tara," he added, crossing his arms across his chest, brooking no disagreement from the 'human.'

"I am happy to bow to your expertise, as I enjoy learning from my elders," I smiled, acknowledging his seniority of being over a hundred human years old.

"You and other 'huumans' state that the Tuatha Dé Danann are the old faery people of Ireland, and that's not quite right," the professor began his account. "They are our distant ancestors, from when the Earth was a misty place, in an historical period that humans call Lemurian. At that time, the veils between the human and elemental worlds were very thin, allowing humans and Tuatha Dé Danann to travel to each other's worlds. This communication did not end in Lemuria and, wherever there were the right conditions—as in the west of Ireland even up to recently—the two races could visit each other's worlds."

"How are the Tuatha Dé Danann related to elementals?' I asked hoarsely, wanting to understand his viewpoint better.

"I was just gettin' to that," he responded, peering at me over his bifocals. "Elementals, like humans, are divided into many races including elves, leprechauns, gnomes, et…cet…era. The closest relatives to the Tuatha Dé Danann are our royal elves. From the Tuatha Dé Danann our royal elves inherited beauty, grace, and even many so-called 'magical powers', not to mention that they think of themselves as the rulers of all the elementals." Lloyd the Grand raised his nose in the air with mock snobbishness during his account of the royal elves.

"Now, I wouldn't be sayin' that these nobles were as smart as some of the rest of us, nor as rich." He doubled up, chortling with glee, because elves often need to borrow money from clever leprechauns. Pulling himself together, he said, "As the Tuatha Dé Danann began to die out, and in order to preserve their culture, they interbred with primitive, less developed, elementals. Our current race of elementals—hybrids, you call them—was the result."

"That is similar to what happened with the Lemurian and Atlantean ancestors of humans," I interjected. "When the Lemurians and Atlanteans began to die out they interbred with primitive humans to raise the consciousness of the humans. These hybrid children were called the sons and daughters of the gods. The Irish heroes, Cuchulainn and Fionn MacCumhaill (pronounced Finn MacCool), were hybrid sons of these Atlantean gods."

"So they were. Anyway, back to the elementals," the leprechaun responded, cutting me off and eager to resume *his* story. "Queen Maeve comes from the Tuatha Dé Danann bloodline; that's why she was known as the Queen of the Faeries. Her home was at Tara. When the Tuatha Dé Danann were fadin', they handed over their site of power to the sons of the gods, the Atlanteans, who were yer mythical Kings of Tara."

Our conversation came to an abrupt end when he pulled a gigantic pocket watch out of his jacket, looked at it in shock, and exclaimed,

"Bless the Craic, I'm late! Time to get back to the others, as they're ready to go through Newgrange. Yer the lucky one who can visit Newgrange, while yer lyin' nice and snug in bed."

After my friend's hurried departure, I reflected on his remarks. Since meeting him, my experience of time and space had changed dramatically. It no longer seemed necessary to go anywhere physically, for I could re-experience previous tours and pilgrimages merely by reflection.

As these thoughts flickered through my mind, I thought about the last time I'd been at Newgrange. Closing my eyes, I immediately saw the gigantic mound encased in white quartz crystal, as it had appeared 5000 years ago when it was first built. Newgrange is associated with the Tuatha Dé Danann, and is said to have been built by their chief god Dagda and his wife Boann, from whom comes the name for the river Boyne. Tradition has it that their son Oengus, the god of love, lived in Newgrange.

One of the joys of taking a group to Newgrange is having private time to meditate in the deep, dark silence inside the central chamber. It is like meditating in the total darkness of the Kings Chamber of the Pyramid of Giza in Egypt. Both places are doorways to other dimensions, other times, other lives, and you can feel the tangible presence of the Otherworld in them. I have always felt fortunate to have permission to lead meditations at sacred sites, as they are both transformative for the individuals participating in them and beneficial for the Earth. I was reminded of my good fortune during my last tour to Newgrange.

On that other tour, we first met our guide Meredith, an archaeologist and reciter of Yeats' poetry, at Newgrange. She was slender, of medium height, with sandy brown hair, and the otherworldly gaze of someone interested in Ireland's mystical poet, Yeats, who—not by coincidence, I think—recorded stories of faeries a hundred years ago.

When I mentioned to Meredith that I had requested private meditation time, she said dubiously, "I don't think you'll be able to get it. I'm an Irish guide, and even I can't get private time for my groups."

"We've already received permission," I stated, pulling out my paper to show her.

"That's amazing. Maybe it's because you're from abroad," Meredith murmured to herself, obviously not pleased that foreigners could get what a local Irish lass could not. In her place, I probably would have had the same reaction.

"It's not just at Newgrange," I explained, trying to still the waters. "On most of our tours and pilgrimages we receive permission for private meditations. I believe it is the Earth, herself, who sees to this, as our main purpose is to open the energy points of the Earth to heal her."

"That's fascinating," she responded with warmth. "I don't think I've ever met a group like yours before. I'll enjoy being your guide for the next few days."

At that moment, a staff member from Newgrange signalled us to commence walking towards the entrance and we quickly stepped into line. We passed by the spiral symbols honouring the Earth Goddess that are carved on the large stones guarding the entrance. Bending over, so as not to bump our heads, we walked in stooped position down the narrow, central passageway lined by more stones with spiral reliefs. Behind us, we heard one of our members attempting to turn around to go back out. Not everyone can take the claustrophobic feeling of the tunnel and inner chamber.

Newgrange

The passageway ended with three chambers off a central chamber. Round stone basins, which originally held ritual offerings, sat in each of the three alcoves. No human bones dating from the time of its construction have been found, as Newgrange, contrary to some people's beliefs, was not originally intended as a place to bury people. So, then, what was the purpose of Newgrange?

I believe that it was an initiation chamber to move people through a spiritual death to a rebirth. Dawn, on the twenty-first day of December, the winter solstice, is the most powerful time at Newgrange. On that day, the rays of the rising sun travel through a hole in a roof box at the entrance, and down the nineteen-metre passageway to illuminate the chamber for about fifteen minutes. That this event still occurs

5000 years after the construction of the site attests to the remarkable astronomic knowledge of the builders of Newgrange.

Looking up from the central chamber, I saw the corbelled beehive roof, unaltered since its construction, soaring some six metres above the ground. This roof reminded me of the conical hats that Tibetan monks wear to attract spiritual energies, suggesting the same purpose at Newgrange, and of the hat that Lloyd wore at our ritual at St. Brigid's Well.

When everyone had arrived in the central chamber, we meditated silently in complete darkness to honour Newgrange and the people who had built it, and whose presence we still felt. These guardians are what remain of the etheric memories of the powerful spiritual leaders who built Newgrange and the later Kings of Tara. These etheric memories remain in sacred sites to protect them, and it is important to honour both the sites and their guardians. Sacred sites are not just tourist attractions. They have powerful energies that can be used for good, or not for good, depending on the individual visiting them and also on the etheric memories of the site.

That day in Newgrange, having finished the meditation, Meredith and I quietly retraced our steps back out.

"That was a remarkable experience," Meredith said, pleased that she had joined in.

We spent the next few days visiting the lesser-known megalithic monuments of Sligo with her. At the end of our time together, we were having a final lunch, when Meredith approached me.

"I'd like to join you for the rest of the tour. Could I do this, if I pay my own accommodation and food?"

"Of course, you are welcome," I laughed, in response to her question, recalling that many guides in the past have joined our entire tour for the sheer pleasure of joining in with the almost magical experiences.

"But you don't have any clothes," I mentioned.

"Not to worry. I'll wash out my underwear at night and Colleen (one of our group members) said she'd lend me another sweater. I just need to call my husband to tell him that I'm off with you for the next three days."

With those words, she walked to a phone box and made a call. Fifteen minutes later we re-boarded the bus accompanied by our newest tour member, Meredith.

Smiling in remembrance of that earlier tour, I opened my eyes and was relieved to see that I was alone in the hotel room. What a luxury to have time to reflect on what I was learning from our pilgrimage. Meditating, doing rituals, and asking for transformation at sacred sites like Newgrange and the Hill of Tara invite universal consciousness, the Holy Spirit, the Craic (by yet another name) to do anything it wants to transform us. Although it is sometimes unpleasant, as the others and I had learned, it is necessary to be cracked open, like a seed, in order to grow into who we truly are.

Life can be either an outer tour, as in the detached way tourists visit sites, or an inner tour allowing events, people, and places to grow us. We can choose which tour to take. Whereas Meredith with her love of spirit had chosen to take the inner tour, Michael, Paddy, and Brian, believing only what they saw in the material world, were taking the outer tour at this time in their lives. But this could change for them or anyone, at another time or place, for all that is required is a shift in intention and perspective. Perhaps a seed of possibilities about elementals and deeper meaning of sacred sites was planted in them on our tour that would blossom later. I have witnessed this happening, both in others and myself, too many times ever to judge divine timing.

"Oh well, it is as it is," I thought to myself, accepting what I could not change. Gazing at the clock, I noticed that it was afternoon so I called the desk to see if my toiletries bag and clothes had arrived. After all, my possessions were supposed to have come in one, not three, days.

"They are at the Dublin airport," the clerk replied to my question. "They should be at the hotel by tonight."

Perhaps because of the good news, or because I started to feel better, the phone beside my bed rang at that moment.

"We've got a problem," Ruth said, after I answered the phone. "Brian told the group that the dinners in Dublin aren't included and people are upset because it says on the brochure that they paid for them."

"Yes, they have paid," I squeezed out in a raspy voice. "I'll call James."

Chuckling to myself with renewed Irish humour, I hung up. My two days of rest appeared to be over as the Craic had reclaimed us. I phoned James the Lep to discover that he'd been working on the situation.

"I've called Margaret, our travel agent in Canada, and you're right, you have paid for all the dinners," he said before adding, "Sorry for the inconvenience."

I conveyed James' apology to our group at supper. Nevertheless, more damage to our credibility had occurred. Gazing around the room at my fellow pilgrims, I noticed that they had split into three camps. The first camp had converted to the Craic and was treating each new experience with amusement. This group was taking the inner as well as the outer tour. The second camp was not amused and, along with Michael and Paddy, was looking for someone to blame, and flipped back and forth between Gallows Tours and me. The third camp could be called confused. Although these individuals reacted negatively, when encountering any new unpleasant Craic experience, given time, they regained their equilibrium and good humour.

Various parts of me could identify with all three groups. But most times, when faced with yet another bend in the road, I was now able to stay in what I call the 'neutral-positive'. 'Neutral' is accepting what is and 'positive' is trusting spirit that the ultimate outcome will be good for our inner transformation.

My illness had gifted me with this neutral-positive outlook, as I had no energy left to continue to try to change 'what is'. I realized that our greatest difficulties in life, whether an illness, loss of a job, loss of a loved one, or loss of anything that we cling too, offer us the greatest opportunity for deep transformation. When we are cracked open, as many of us were, from what on the outside could be viewed as the tour from hell, the light of spirit emerges.

Deep in contemplation, and still unable to speak with my fellow pilgrims above a hoarse whisper, I excused myself from dinner and retired for the night. I needed more sleep to recover, because tomorrow was the final day of the pilgrimage.

chapter twelve

Druids, Uisneagh, and Anam Cara

In the morning my toiletries and clothes had still not arrived. Surprise, surprise! I called James to see what was happening.

"I've got some bad news," he responded. "Because the parcel was sent from Northern Ireland and no one identified it at the Dublin airport, it's been sent back to the hotel in Belleek. In the South they're always worried about a bomb when things are shipped from Northern Ireland."

"Blessed Mary!" I thought to myself. "Even my toiletries have gone into the Craic."

"I'll have your stuff sent to the hotel where you're staying on your next tour," James the Lep offered.

You can imagine how much confidence I had that I'd ever see my own toothbrush. Still, what was there to do, but to accept 'what is', yet again.

"Fine. Thanks for sending them," I said to James, amused to see how my previous expectations had fallen away. I discovered that the more I accepted James just as he was, the more my heart opened to him. Rather than thinking of him as a problem, I had begun to regard him as an ally who was helping me to learn important lessons in unconditional love and acceptance.

Hanging up the phone, I readied myself for our last day.

James had reminded me that I had another tour starting tomorrow and I could only hope that the elementals would then give me time off for good behaviour. I was using another company, which specialized in trekking, and half of the eighteen hikers would be the shell-shocked pilgrims from our present trip. Let's face it: I also was no longer in the best physical or emotional shape of my life. Willing myself back to the present moment, I picked up my room keys and went down for breakfast.

It's customary to give tips to the guide and bus driver on the last day so I made the rounds to collect for Michael and Paddy. We had another guide who specialized on Dublin and, therefore, Michael was leaving us after breakfast. While our weary travellers filed onto the bus for the city tour, I approached Michael who was standing at the entrance of the hotel saying his goodbyes.

"Thank you for staying with us. I know it wasn't easy and I appreciate it," I said, accepting his extended hand.

"Well, it's fine," replied Michael, in as positive a manner as he could muster given how exhausted he must have been with all he had gone through psychologically.

"This is to show our appreciation," I said, handing him our card and envelope of contributions.

Knowing that money alone could never make up for the stress he had encountered, I'd put in some extra. I had received a wonderful gift through my journey in the Craic and felt sad that Paddy, Michael, and Brian had not learned these same lessons. Although I could be mistaken, I do not think that they had ever left the stormy surface of the tour to discover the many pearls of wisdom on the sea floor. All of them had given me subtle, and not so subtle, feedback that they had no intention of diving into the depths.

If our tour had been made into a Hollywood movie, the scriptwriter would have wanted Paddy and Michael to become believers in leprechauns and we'd all have become the best of friends. However, real life doesn't always have a happy ending full of rainbows. In real life the story continues after the lights in the theatre come on, and I was hopeful that, because of our journey together, deep changes were occurring in Paddy, Michael, and Brian that would bear fruit at a later date. On the surface level, the best on which the four of us could agree was that we had held the tour 'somewhat' together by employing goodwill and flexibility. I felt immense gratitude for this gift.

Following our Dublin tour, folks split up to do last–minute shopping. Not fully recovered, I left them to their pleasures and returned to the hotel for a nap before our final meeting at five pm. I had just climbed into bed when the leprechaun appeared.

"Tyin' up loose ends. I'm almost done," he mumbled to himself, while pacing back and forth across the room.

"What are you talking about?" I inquired, pulling the covers up around my neck.

"We still haven't spoken about Druids and Uisneagh," he replied, heaving his chunky little body into the armchair.

"Then we'd best get on with it," I said, accepting the inevitable and realizing that my nap was not going to happen anytime soon.

"Why are the Druids important to elementals?" I nudged my friend, wanting to understand why we needed to talk about them anyway.

"The Tuatha Dé Danann, and, later, we elementals, were the *teachers* of the Druids," stressed my pal, eager as always to show the importance of elementals to humans. "It is no word of a lie that, because of us, the Druids and their predecessors lived in harmony with nature for thousands of years."

"I know a little about them," I jumped in, engaging my chum in his favourite pastime—playing the 'who-knows-the-most' game with the 'human'. "The name 'Druid' means a *'wise holder of knowledge'*, and there were three levels in their system. The first level was a *Filidh* who knew law, medicine, and astronomy. Bards, the second level, were singers and poets who could recite twenty thousand verses of oral poetry. Did you know that their memory was believed to be twenty times greater than that of humans today?"

"Humans would have better memories if they used 'em instead of always doin' everythin' on 'em computers," Lloyd interjected, taking a crack at one of his pet peeves, technology. "We elementals didn't have a whole lot to do with the *Filidh* except for teachin' them about plant medicines. But we certainly were busy with those Bards—poetry, storytellin', and music bein' our expertise and all."

"Did elementals have much to do with the third level—the ones actually called the Druids?" I asked. "From what I've learned, they studied the natural and spiritual world for twenty years in order to become the spiritual custodians of their people. Evidently, they seldom married and lived in abstinence in a community, secluded cave, or forest dwelling. Although many could write Ogham, Greek, and later, Latin, they kept their Druidic lore secret and did not commit it to writing."

"Everythin' you say about them is spot on. Elementals taught Druids about natural laws, and Druids taught us the spiritual laws. So there was a good bit of reciprocity goin' on. Did you know that Druids had a Virgin Mother and that they also believed in reincarnation?" my friend asked, eager to demonstrate his knowledge of human history.

"I did," I responded.

"I'll tell you somethin' you didn't know," he said, smiling mischievously. "Their main centre at Uisneagh Hill is the very heart of Ireland."

"That makes sense energetically, as the meeting point of the five ancient kingdoms of Ireland was at Uisneagh," I replied, not sure why he wanted to talk about Uisneagh, as our pilgrims had not visited that site. The site is on private land, and it is too dangerous and difficult to take a group there as you must go through fields occupied by sheep and cattle and over many barbed-wire fences to get to it. For this reason, Uisneagh remains virtually unknown.

"I can't put anythin' over on you, can I?" my elemental comrade laughed. "I was warmin' you up to tell of yer first time in Uisneagh."

"I'd rather not; it's too personal," I replied, embarrassed by how my sneaky friend had worked me into a corner. How did he know about my experience? I certainly hadn't told him!

"You don't need to tell me 'cos it's written all over yer energy pattern, so that even an elemental baby could read it. You are too secretive by half—too many lives as a Druid. You've kept yer knowledge safe, but this secrecy must end as you are blockin' the energy in yer throat. No wonder you can't speak. The only lastin' cure is to tell yer personal stories about yer heart wounds. So go on, tell what you did at Uisneagh."

"Just a minute now, who is calling the kettle black?" I retorted, defending my right to privacy. "Leprechauns are renowned for their secrecy."

"I'd not be sayin' that I didn't have the same problem as you," he asserted, holding up his hands in a conciliatory gesture. "In fact, all Irish are just like divils with their secrets. However, that bein' as it is, we elementals are takin' a big risk exposin' ourselves through yer books in an attempt to reach more humans. You have to take some risks in exposin' yerself, or you'll never carry as much energy as you are capable of. Our entire pilgrimage in Ireland was meant to shed light on folk's dark places so that they could give 'em up. As you see, we're right on topic with you me girl. So start talkin'!"

"Very well," I began shyly, realizing the truth of his words. "The great festival of Beltane, lasting from May 1st to May 15th, took place at the giant dolmen at Uisneagh. Uisneagh was well-known in the ancient world, and traders from as far away as the Mediterranean brought silks and spices to the festival."

Ail na Mearainn at Uisneagh

"The dolmen, called *Ail na Mearainn* in Irish, is smack dab on those energy lines that we were talkin' about," said the leprechaun, lending me encouragement. "So if you could just recount what you did there..."

"I was with a man whom I loved deeply and I believed him to be not only my lover, but also my soul friend, my *Anam Cara* (literally *friend of the soul* in Irish). We made love on top of the stone, which, after all, is the traditional way to celebrate Beltane. It was a fierce blow to my heart when he left, as he did not honour our deeper Anam Cara relationship."

"It's a terrible thing to lose yer Anam Cara," said my pal, amazingly sympathetic. "It's happened to me. An Anam Cara is not necessarily a sexual relationship, although it might be as in yer case. My Anam Cara was not sexual. He was an elf, and we were amongst the first elementals to work in human-elemental partnerships to help the Earth.

Together we did so much in the beginning, but he could not stay the course. He left because he missed the beautiful elfin life with his own people. Leprechauns, as you know, like to keep to themselves, so it was a great shock when he left our work and me after I'd let him into me inner sanctum. It's hard to trust after you've been betrayed, but that's what I do with you and humans are even harder to trust than elves, who are elementals, at least."

With my friend's words, I realized that he also was my Anam Cara, my soul friend. An Anam Cara could be a man or woman, or even a being like my elemental friend from another race. It is someone who is destined to enter your life even though you might not know the significance at the time. An Anam Cara helps you across a threshold to a deeper awakening and unconditional love, while you do the same for him or her.

You might have only one Anam Cara in a lifetime, but sometimes we are fortunate to have more than one. These soul relationships transcend time and space. Even if the person leaves or dies, or you spend little time with him or her, your Anam Cara still holds a special place in your heart. Perhaps, it is someone you recognize from a past life, or a fellow journeyer on the spiritual path. I am fortunate to have had a few Anam Cara in my life, however, the loss of a beloved with whom you have shared your heart is especially painful.

"That, me friend," said the wise leprechaun, having heard all my thoughts and reservations, "is why you've had to tell the story again now. It's all a matter of energy. If you don't commit yer energy to the story, how can you be healed to the same depth as yer original woundin'? What is done at sacred sites—rituals and the like and especially those using sexual energy—creates an incredibly powerful impact on yer etheric body, which is yer body elemental that holds all your memories in yer cells. That's why it has taken so long to heal."

"I understand this," I replied vulnerably. "It's just that I'd much prefer either to deal with this privately, or to speak of it only with another soul friend."

"Of course, you would," said the leprechaun, breaking into gales of laughter at my discomfort. "But, this isn't just yer story. This is the story of everyone who has been hurt by the loss of his or her Anam Cara and of everyone who yearns for a soul friend. Yer story is a story of healin' for others as well as yerself. The last lesson that we've been teachin' you on our pilgrimage is to keep yer heart open to love unconditionally no matter what happens. Love is somethin' elementals learn from humans, and you've given it to me. Now I give it right back to you."

I knew Lloyd was correct and that unconditional love was once again required. The bottomless pit of the Craic was now into my deepest personal areas. Speaking of the experience has taken me through memories of love and despair, finally to feelings of gratitude and amusement at my own melodrama.

"Don't be so hard on yerself," my pal said gently, "You've continued to love and trust us elementals even though we've made it difficult and most of the 'huuumans' on the tour have done this as well. It's not one-sided, you know? Some of our elementals, who were a wee bit unsure about trustin' humans, have a deeper respect and appreciation for humans now 'cos we've watched yer folks go through the pain of the Craic and get right back up. We are seeking human partners to commit to us elementals and we've found 'em, which gives us hope that together we can heal the Earth. Many Anam Cara relationships have formed during our pilgrimage."

My friend's words touched my heart, but before I could wax nostalgic, my pal ever quick to change a mood, rubbing his hands together signalling a job well done, chirped up with, "That's enough fer now. It's time to get ready for our meetin' and fare-thee-well and— there might be a slight problem."

Dragging my body out of bed, I threw on some clothes and raced down the hall. Our get-together was to commence in ten minutes and, arriving at the room, I discovered that it had not been set up as I had requested. Rather than a circle of chairs in a neat room, I was flabbergasted to see boardroom tables littered with dirty dishes.

"Told ya," my leprechaun co-leader said, sitting down on the nearest chair, making it clear that he was not intending to help.

"How did you jump to that conclusion?" he said, in mock exasperation at my thought. "I've got elementals standin' by for the fare-thee-well and right now there's two of yer folks on their way to lend a hand. I suggest you git someone from the front desk to clean up here," he directed, waving his hand to indicate the mess.

Just then Ruth and Ralph arrived. Seeing the situation, and without being asked, my saviours started moving the boardroom tables to the side of the room and setting the chairs in a circle. I located a phone and called the front desk to ask them to send someone to remove the dirty dishes. A young man showed up soon afterwards and, by the time the majority of the group had appeared in their dress-up clothes, the room was ready for them. Oh, what goes on behind the scenes!

The humans took a seat in the circle, and the elementals that had accompanied us on our pilgrimage, also dressed in their best clothes, lined up behind them. I couldn't help but notice that even the elementals looked exhausted.

"I should say so," said my fellow tour director, reading my mind. "It wasn't easy truckin' a load of humans around for eleven days. Still, I'd say we made a fair bit of progress helpin' yer humans with the Craic."

"Let's agree that you've done a great job taking them into the Craic," I replied. "Whether some of them have come out again is yet to be seen."

"You might have a point there," the leprechaun agreed, peering around the room and noting a few sour faces. Some pilgrims looked resigned, but others, praise the powers that be, actually showed signs of enjoyment.

"You see, they've got it," my comrade commented, nodding towards some happy faces. "Others will get it…given time. Anyway, we've planted the Craic seed, fertilized, and watered it. So we've done our job," he said, crossing his arms across his chest and brooking no contradiction.

"Yes we have," I agreed with him, feeling a deep sense of rightness in the purposeful chaos that we had experienced. My elemental colleague was taking credit for creating opportunities to learn and I wanted him to know that 'the human' was taking credit for steering the pilgrimage through those choppy waters. "Shouldn't Brian and James get credit as well?" I asked my friend, amused that my black Irish humour had reasserted itself.

"That they should. We elementals would never have been able to create such great Craic, if they hadn't given us such a mess with which to work. Yes indeed, we should toast 'em tonight."

By now everyone was seated in a circle. I rose from my chair, and walking towards the altar in the centre, lit our final candle. Not having been with the group for several days, I felt somewhat distant from them. They had journeyed to Glendalough, the Hill of Tara, and Newgrange, while I had undergone my own inner journey in bed. I was returning from the experience changed and, because the transformation was still underway, I felt emotionally and spiritually vulnerable. Also, because it was physically so difficult to speak, I had had virtually no conversation with my fellow pilgrims for days. Even now my constricted throat emitted only hoarse whispers after great effort. My heart yearned to connect and to hear what the trip had meant for each of them. With that thought, I passed the pouch for my fellow pilgrims to take their final angel cards.

Molly, her arm not fully healed, was one of the first to speak, "The tour very much had a will of its own. My experiences and insights in Ireland are life changing and I can use them now to guide me in my choices. Quite amazing and beautiful."

Molly's goblin partner, multi-coloured ribbons dangling from his silky top, stood on his best behaviour behind her chair. On his head was a hat, so reminiscent of a jester's, that I had a revelation about how clever goblins have influenced human jesters and wise fools. "Perhaps, Shakespeare had a direct line!" I mused.

Hearing my thought, a wide grin stole across the goblin's face, "So you finally understand how goblins have been helpin' humans," he said indulgently.

The pouch passed to Marion, "I had a wonderful, unforgettable time visiting so many places and having so many adventures, which I will always remember," she said, smiling happily, as pleased as on the day she had climbed Croagh Patrick. The two teenage trolls who had accompanied Marion on her pilgrimage had backed into a corner seemingly overwhelmed by so many humans in such tight quarters.

"And you two?" I asked the trolls telepathically.

Pleased to be noticed by an adult, even a human one, the larger troll, clutching his sapling walking stick in an immense hand, stood up straighter. He was dressed in raggedy pants that came to just below his knees from which hairy legs and gigantic bare feet emerged. His concession to dressing for our final evening was slicking his hair behind his ears with what could have been bear grease. Looking at his elemental elders for approval, he replied in a bass voice employing a few well-chosen words, "Me brother and I had good Craic."

Peggy was next and fortunately her head wound appeared to be completely healed. I eagerly awaited what she had to say about her 'unorthodox' spiritual experiences. "This tour has opened me to an understanding of other worlds and a whole spiritual universe...which includes elementals," she said giggling, as if surprised at her own words. Little Sweetie, standing beside Peggy's chair, looked pleased as punch with 'her human' and many of her diminutive elemental companions nudged each other and smiled. Peggy had made lots of friends on the tour.

Max had been very quiet since his outbreak on Achill Island, and I had absolutely no idea if he had had the worst, or dare we hope, the best tour of his life. Rising from his chair, he approached me with a gift in his hand. It was an old print of Keel done at the turn of the twentieth century. What a touching thought, and so like the man I've come to know as having a soft and generous heart.

"I've learned," Max said, "that I don't need to take responsibility for other people's stuff and this is BIG. Also, I had such a wonderful time in Glendalough that I'm thinking maybe there's something to this elemental stuff."

Another "hurrah" was expressed by the elementals in support of Max.

At this point, Dr. Carl took the pouch, and true to his scientific scholarly nature, expounded about his amazing discovery. "The spirals on the kerbstone at the entrance to Newgrange are a sound scale that works to harmonize the body," he began and continued for a goodly amount of time giving the data on his scientific findings, until finally he noticed that he'd lost his fellow travellers.

Ending on a more personal note, Dr. Carl added, "I had an awakening of deep secrets related to the Christ and also," he paused, and added with a conspiratorial smile, "I was fascinated by the events that were not the advertised part of the trip."

The slender, serious elf, who was a scholar in elfin realms, stood behind Dr. Carl. He was dressed impeccably in black, an unusual colour for an elemental, which further accentuated his solemn, slender appearance. The elf calmly viewed the proceedings and, although pleasant, did not deign to speak with me at that time. He, like Dr. Carl, was committed to working with others to benefit the Earth, but, given their druthers, the two would probably prefer to be alone doing research.

Katje, Dr. Carl's wife, took over at that moment and her thoughts reinforced his last remark. "For me, the most amazing learning was being in the Craic. You must be open the whole time to what is going to happen next, and live in the present without expectations."

Robin, surrounded by small brownies and tiny gnomes, twittering and restless at how slow humans were, decided to speak next. "I am a veteran of many spiritual trips and have ceased to expect that it will be a perfect and fun vacation," she opened. "I learned so much from watching how you handled probably the most difficult on-going situation I have ever seen. It was very different from losing luggage, or not liking your roommate, or people not honouring timeframes. You did a marvellous job of telling it like it was, allowing your own vulnerability to show and most of all, continuing at intervals to hold in front of us the divine laws and principles that were at work in the situation, and guiding-challenging-us to look within ourselves and be observers of our reactions."

Robin's generous comments brought tears to my eyes because I felt deeply seen and understood for what I had attempted to do for my fellow pilgrims. Leaving Robin's hand, the pouch passed from one person to another and I listened closely to what each person had to say. It was gratifying to hear how many mentioned the elementals and the Craic and, like Robin, how many understood that something profound had transpired on our journey. Everyone's sharing touched me and I choose to remember the positive comments because, bless the goddess, they far outweighed any negatives.

My angel card at the beginning of the tour was 'grace' and now I knew through experience that grace was another word for the Craic. Grace is the gift of the Holy Spirit, in whichever form it takes. When my turn came to draw an angel card for what I had learned on the pilgrimage, I drew the card 'joy.' Joy is not the same as happiness. Happiness comes and goes depending on whether our ego's needs are met. Joy, on the other hand, comes from a deep acceptance and satisfaction that one has been the best that one is capable of being. Through my illness I'd realized that I was at my best both for others and myself, when I was compassionately present with all experiences and—astounding to me—without words and without doing.

Meanwhile, my leprechaun pal who was representing the elementals waited eagerly for his angel card. Lloyd's card on the first day of the trip had been 'simplicity,' and if we had received his 'simple' tour, I wondered with amusement what a complex one would have been like. Reaching into the pouch I pulled out the card for what he and the elementals had achieved. It was 'patience.' He threw an 'I told you so' look in my direction and the elementals laughed and nodded in their agreement with him.

The angel card for the group of 'humans' at the beginning of the tour had been 'clarity' and Katje now chose a new card for what we, as a group, had achieved. The new card was 'inspiration.' In the dictionary the word inspiration is defined as 'Divine influence exerted upon the mind'. That is exactly what had happened on our pilgrimage of transformation. Everything, as always, was perfect.

"Of course, everythin' is perfect. What else would it be?" said Lloyd.

Gazing around the room, I silently thanked all the elementals who had accompanied us on our journey. The elves acknowledged my gratitude with graceful bows and curtsies; leprechauns raised their hats smiling; little gnomes and brownies twittered in glee; and even the goblins smirked in their form of a smile. The elementals appeared stronger, both physically and in their sense of self, than at the beginning of our tour, as working with the humans had transformed them as well. Instead of having thirty pilgrims, there had really been sixty of us.

The 'humans' got up from their chairs to leave for our farewell dinner, and simultaneously, the elementals disappeared. For the elementals, the tour had ended.

"Not yet!" retorted my leprechaun co-leader. "I thought we could talk about our *next* tour. I'm just getting' into the swing of it now."

"What next tour?" I responded surprised.

My chum sent me an image of 'Himself' dressed as a pharaoh, complete with a headdress reminiscent of King Tutankhamen. The major difference was a live cobra on my friend's headdress that swayed from side to side, glaring at me. Extending his arm in a great show of ceremony, the leprechaun unrolled a papyrus scroll with a flourish. On it was written *Pilgrimage of Egypt for Humans*.

A look of horror must have crossed my face, as I thought of what the leprechaun could do with the Craic in Egypt, because my irrepressible friend immediately collapsed in howls of laughter and, catching my eye, winked and disappeared.

p.s.

Since writing my last book *Summer with the Leprechauns* I have met thousands of humans and elementals who are committed to working together to become co-creators and guardians of the Earth. My hope is that those of you who have read this story and accompanied us on the pilgrimage will want to join us. As you can see, it is not for the faint-hearted, but there are always elementals waiting to welcome wayshowers of love and light into their band as co-creators on our beautiful planet. They are there when you walk in the forest, when you garden, and when you allow the Craic into your life. They are there.

Keys to Flowing
with the Craic
by the Leprechaun

1 Do not resist. Resistance is futile.
2 Open yourself fully and embrace the lessons of the Craic.
3 To recognize the lessons of the Craic, observe your stuck places where you feel angry, self-pitying, frustrated, blaming.
4 Experiences with the Craic never end. When you have learned one lesson, another lesson will be presented for you to learn.
5 Do not pass the buck. If you are triggered, you have something to learn.
6 Take a moment to celebrate the teachers of good Craic. You're lucky to know them.
7 The Craic comes in many guises. Light Craic is amusing, while dark Craic is provoking, and the two often come in the same package.
8 Try humour when in doubt of your best approach.
9 When humour does not work, become non-attached to the outcome and accept 'what is'.
10 Enjoy your life in the present moment. Trying to escape to the past or future will only tie you in a tighter knot.

Lessons from the pilgrimage by the 'human'

1 You can't always get what you want, but if you try sometimes, you will find that you get what you ne-ee-ee-ed.

2 Be grateful for the gifts you receive daily from spirit, referred to by Christians as grace, and by the Irish and elementals as the Craic.

3 These gifts often lie beyond your known limits physically, psychologically, or spiritually.

4 Trust spirit, the Craic, and others as much as you trust yourself.

5 Pain is a part of life and one of the greatest ways in which we learn. Even in the midst of joy and plenty, pain is never far away.

6 Non-attachment to getting what you want is the quickest way of releasing pain.

7 Have no expectations about how spirit and the Craic will teach you their lessons.

8 Accept 'what is' in others and in situations you encounter. This is the key to inner peace.

9 Light Craic is laughing at yourself and seeing humour in difficult situations.

10 Ask others for help when you need it and welcome their gifts gratefully.

11 Remain in 'neutral-positive' when faced with difficulties. Neutral is being unattached to the outcome; positive is trusting that spirit has good intentions towards you.

12 Keep your heart open to love unconditionally, no matter what happens.

Further Reading on Nature Spirits

Arrowsmith, Nancy (with George Moorse), *A Field Guide to the Little People*, McMillan, London, 1977.

Evans-Wentz, W,Y., *The Fairy Faith in Celtic Countries* (1911), University Books, New York, 1977.

Froud Brian (with Abu Lee), *Faeries*, Harry Abrams Inc., New York, 1978.

Huygen (ill. Rien Poortvliet) *Gnomes*, Harry Abrams Inc., New York, 1977.

Helliwell, Tanis, *Summer with the Leprechauns: A True Story*, 1997.

Hodson, Geoffrey, *Faeries at Work and Play*, Theosophical Publishing House, Wheaton, IL

Gregory, Lady, *Visions and Beliefs in the West of Ireland* (1920), Gerrards Cross, Snythe, 1970.

MacLean Dorothy, *To Hear the Angels Sing*, Lorian Press, 1980.

MacNamara, Niall, (ill. Wayne Anderson), *Leprechaun Companion*, Pavillon Books, London, 1999.

MacManus, Diamuid, *Irish Earth Folk*, The Devin-Adair Company, New York, 1988.

Megre, Vladimir, *The Ringing Cedar Series of 8*, Ringing Cedars Press, 2000.

Papenfus, Stan, *Paddy's Chin*, Life Cycle Centre, Ireland, 2003.

Pogacnik, Marko, *Nature Spirits & Elemental Beings*, Findhorn Press, Forres, Scotland, 2004.

Michael J. Roads, *Journey into Nature*, HJ Kramer Inc., Tiburon, CA 1990.

Rose, Carol, *Spirits, Fairies, Leprechauns, and Goblins*, Norton, New York, 1996.

Small Wright, Machelle, *Behaving as if God in all Life Mattered*, Perelandra, Warrenton, VA, 1987.

Tompkins, Peter, *The Secret Life of Nature*, HarperCollins, New York, 1997.

Von Gilder, Dora, *Fairies*, Quest Books, Wheaton, IL, 1994.

Yeats, W.B., *Fairy and the Folk Tales of the Irish Peasantry* (1888) and *Irish Fairy Tales* (1892) reprinted SmithMark Publ., New York, 1996.

Further Reading on Pilgrimage

Chatwin, Bruce, *The Songlines*, Penguin, NY, 1998.

Coelho, Paulo, *The Pilgrimage*, Harper SanFrancisco, Ca, 1995.

Cousineau, Phil, *The Art of Pilgrimage*, Conari Press, Boston, 1998.

Foster, Barbara & Michael, *Forbidden Journey, The Life of Alexandra David-Neel*, Harper & Row, SanFrancisco, 1987.

Galland, China, *Longing for Darkness: Tara and the Black Madonna*, Penguin, NY, 1990.

Lozano, Millan Bravo, *A Practical Guide for Pilgrims: The Road to Santiago*, Editorial Everest, 1999.

MacLaine, Shirley, *The Camino*, Pocket Books, NY, 2000.

Milne, Courtney, *The Sacred Earth*, Viking Penguin, NY, 1991.

Peace Pilgrim, *Peace Pilgrim*, Ocean Tree, Santa Monica, Ca, 1994.

About the Author

Tanis Helliwell M.Ed. is the founder of the International Institute for Transformation (IIT), which offers programs to assist individuals to become conscious creators to work with the spiritual laws that govern our world.

Tanis Helliwell is the author of *Summer with the Leprechauns: A True Story, Take Your Soul to Work,* a book of poetry called *Embraced by Love,* and *Decoding Your Destiny: Keys to Humanity's Spiritual Evolution.* She is a student and teacher of the Inner Mysteries, living on the seacoast north of Vancouver, Canada. For over twenty years, she has led people on tours and walking pilgrimages to sacred sites in Egypt, Israel, Peru, Bolivia, India, Nepal, France, Britain, Scotland, Ireland, the American Southwest, New Zealand, Japan, Kenya, and Greece.

Since childhood, she has seen and heard elementals, angels, and master teachers on other planes. For sixteen years she conducted a therapy practice, helping people with their spiritual transformation.

In addition to her spiritual workshops, she is a sought-after keynote speaker and has worked for almost thirty years as a consultant to businesses, universities, and government, both to create healthy organizations and to help people develop their personal and professional potential.

Her work is committed to helping people to develop right relationships with themselves, others and the Earth.

To write to the author, order books, CDs, and DVDs, or for information on upcoming tours and workshops, please contact:

Tanis Helliwell
C4 Hollingsworth Rd., RR #3 Powell River, BC., Canada V8A 5C1
E-mail: tanis@tanishelliwell.com
Web site: www.tanishelliwell.com

BOOKS:
Pilgrimage with the Leprechauns: a true story of a mystical tour of Ireland CDN $21.95
Summer with the Leprechauns: a true story CDN $20
Take Your Soul to Work CDN $20
Embraced by Love CDN $15.95
Decoding Your Destiny: Keys to Humanity's Spiritual Evolution CDN $21.95

CDs
Series A - Discovering Yourself: 2 visualizations
1. Path of Your Life / Your Favourite Place
2. Eliminating Negativity / Purpose of Your Life
3. Linking Up World Servers / Healing the Earth

Series B - The Inner Mysteries: talk and visualization
1. Reawakening Ancestral Memory / Between the Worlds
2. The Celtic Mysteries / Quest for the Holy Grail
3. The Egyptian Mysteries / Initiation in the Pyramid of Giza

4. The Greek Mysteries / Your Male and Female Archetypes
5. The Christian Mysteries / Jesus Life: A Story of Initiation
6. Address from the Earth/Manifesting Peace on Earth

Individual CDs   CDN $20
Series A (3 items) CDN $55
Series B (6 items) CDN $105

DVDs:
1. Take Your Soul to Work   CDN $20
2. Managing the Stress of Change CDN $20

plus postage and handling

CPSIA information can be obtained at www.ICGtesting.com
Printed in the USA
LVOW101523221212

312908LV00001B/4/P